STAND UP!
FOR YOURSELF

STAND UP! FOR YOURSELF
Step Toward a New Direction Using Principles

Jennie Msangi

Trilogy Christian Publishers A Wholly Owned Subsidiary of Trinity Broadcasting Network 2442 Michelle Drive Tustin, CA 92780

Copyright © 2020 by Jennie Msangi

No part of this book may be reproduced, stored in a retrieval system or transmitted by any means without written permission from the author. All rights reserved.

Printed in USA

Rights Department, 2442 Michelle Drive, Tustin, CA 92780.

Trilogy Christian Publishing/ TBN and colophon are trademarks of Trinity Broadcasting Network.

For information about special discounts for bulk purchases, please contact Trilogy Christian Publishing.

Trilogy Disclaimer: The views and content expressed in this book are those of the author and may not necessarily reflect the views and doctrine of Trilogy Christian Publishing or the Trinity Broadcasting Network.

Manufactured in the United States of America

10 9 8 7 6 5 4 3 2 1

Library of Congress Cataloging-in-Publication Data is available.

ISBN: 978-1-64088-951-4

E-ISBN: 978-1-64088-952-1

"Now when these things begin to happen, ***stand up*** straight and raise your heads; because your redemption is near."

Luke 21:28 CEB

DEDICATION

I would like to dedicate this book to my parents, Sam and Zelma. They have always encouraged me to **Stand Up!** and pursue my dreams. Celebrating more than 67 years of marriage, they are a living testimony to perseverance and living a quality life and not a quantity life.

ACKNOWLEDGMENTS

I would like to thank my husband Gill and children Abbie, Alissa, Apollo, Jasmine, and Mary for their ongoing support. It is through their togetherness as a family, their cooperation, and loving attitudes that I have been able to complete this work and share it with others.

TABLE OF CONTENTS

About Stand Up! 13

Introduction 15

The Foundation of Stand Up! 21

Living by the Momentum 27

Stand Up! Pathways to Overall Wellbeing 37

The Principle of Purpose and Vision 47

The Principle of Faith 53

The Principle of Perseverance 59

The Principle of Togetherness 67

The Principle of Cooperative Work 79

The Principle of Responsibility 87

The Principle of a Loving Attitude 101

The Principle of Resourcefulness 109

The Principle of Self Discipline 123

Time for Action 133

Stand Up! Goal Setting 137

What's Next 147

Appendix.................................. 153

References................................. 159

About The Author............................ 167

ABOUT STAND UP!

Stand Up! *For Yourself and Step Toward a New Direction Using Principles* is an action plan for you to improve your current living situation. *Stand Up!* is dedicated to providing opportunities for you and your family to step toward a new direction by learning and applying the *Stand Up!* principles.

The goals of *Stand Up!* are:

- To motivate you to explore your current situation and then step toward a new direction through the program principles.

- To encourage you to pursue available opportunities to improve your current situations through education and shared resourcing.

- To provide you with appropriate tools, tips, and techniques.

You cannot just read this book. You must participate in it! It is a call to action. As a *Stand Up!* participant, you will:

- Complete the *Stand Up! Quality Living Continuum* to identify your current pathway.
- Develop your personal purpose and vision statement.
- Learn how the nine principles apply in your life.
- Identify your strengths, supports, and resources.
- Develop a 10–80–10 spending plan.
- Complete the *Stand Up! Health Awareness Appraisal*.
- Complete the *Personal Habits Motivation Questionnaire*.
- Identify and track your goals and action steps.
- Begin your daily *Stand Up! Journal*.
- See how you can budget your time more efficiently.
- Track your *Household Responsibility and I See You (ICU)* time.

INTRODUCTION

I have to admit that I had a pretty great childhood. My dad worked hard for our family, and my mother stayed home with my brothers, sister, and me. I did well in school, and I had great friends. We lived in a big, old farmhouse and always had plenty of food and fun. Looking back, I guess we would have fit the definition of working poor, but I never knew it. I never had anything else with which to compare it. Every other family around us seemed to live the same way we did, so I figured that is how life was meant to be, and I was satisfied. So, were we poor? Yes. Did we live poorly? No. And that is what I want you to realize about yourself while you read this book. *Being poor doesn't mean you have to live poorly. Stand Up!* For yourself and seek to live a quality life as you step toward a new direction.

While my four siblings went on to live in the tradition of our childhood, I ended up living in situations where I was exposed to poverty, addiction, violence, and crime. While most of the people I grew up with never left our small town, I have had the opportunity to travel not only throughout the United States but also to travel abroad. I can tell you poor is poor, no matter in what country you are living.

However, I acknowledge that without all of those events, I wouldn't be the person that I am today. Everything I have experienced has led me to this point in my life, and I am thankful that I can pull from those experiences and share some strategies with you in the hopes that if you are in similar situations that you will be able to *Stand Up! For Yourself* and step toward a new direction.

Now, I could choose to state that I was qualified to develop *Stand Up!* because I have a college degree or that I have over thirty years of experience serving families through public service agencies. However, I feel that my true qualifications for developing *Stand Up!* are not based upon the education or experience that I gained in the classroom or office, but upon the education and experience I have gained through living life.

I have raised five children over the course of my life. I have lived on government programs. I have faced eviction because I couldn't pay the rent. I have had to work two or three jobs at a time just to spend most of my paycheck on daycare and gas. I have had to take the bus or walk because I couldn't afford a car (having a luxury car was simply the luxury of actually having a car), or if I did have a car, there were times where I just couldn't afford the insurance or the gas.

I have had to go to churches and social service agencies because my utilities were in jeopardy or I didn't have enough groceries to last or so that my children could have Christmas presents, I have had to shop at thrift stores, flea markets, and dollar stores because I couldn't afford to go anywhere else. Many times, I just had to learn to go without.

I have lived in homes where almost everything I owned was either given to me or I found it at a yard sale or on the curb on trash day. I have had to borrow money from friends and family, knowing that I had no idea of how, if, or when I would pay them back. I have had my phone and cable shut off on more than one occasion.

I have sat at home with my children wishing I could take them someplace nice but not being able to afford it. I have also wished I could go someplace nice myself but wasn't able to afford a babysitter. I have lived through sickness because I couldn't afford the gas to go to the doctor or buy the medicine he prescribed me if I did see him. The list goes on and on.

However, through all of these life events, I managed to survive. But just surviving was not enough for me. I wanted a better life for myself and my family—*I wasn't flourishing, I was floundering*. I needed to get out of the destructive cycle in which I had permitted myself to become trapped. I had to *Stand Up! and Step Toward a New Direction Using Principles*.

And you know what? My story isn't even that bad. Many people have it much worse. If someone has any kind of criminal record, it is next to impossible to find anything besides minimum wage jobs. At that point, choosing a career goes out of the window. They often have to take what they can get for work at that point. They can't even volunteer at most places, and the places designed to help them find employment, most by law, cannot hire them. Now, how can you expect an organization that can't even consider them for employment find success marketing them to someone else? What are they supposed to say to the community, "We won't hire them, but I'm sure they will work great for you!"? In the meantime, they have to eat and pay the bills, so *if society won't let you grow, you go with what you know* causing a perpetual system designed for failure.

Maybe your situation is similar, or yours may be much worse than what I described, but no matter what your situation, you can *Stand Up!* If I can do it, you can do it too! If you find that you are at a crossroads in your life, then it is time. You can apply the biblical principles of *Stand Up!* to achieve quality living.

When you feel like your get up and go has got up and went

When you feel like your time and your money has all been spent

When you feel you're drowning in darkness with no end in sight

It is time to Stand Up! and Step Toward a New Direction

and head toward that light.

The light that only Jesus can provide.

The light that shines on the inside!

Stand Up!

THE FOUNDATION OF STAND UP!

Scripture Ties:

Do not merely listen to the word, and so deceive yourselves. Do what it says. Anyone who listens to the word but does not do what it says is like someone who looks at his face in a mirror and, after looking at himself, goes away and immediately forgets what he looks like.

(James 1:22–24 NIV)

Commit to the Lord whatever you do, and he will establish your plans.

(Proverbs 16:3 NIV)

And be not conformed to this world: but be ye transformed by the renewing of your mind, that ye may prove what is that good, and acceptable, and perfect, will of God.

(Romans 12:2 KJV)

It is important to start by answering the following questions. So, who are you? What are you about? How do you identify yourself? What is your passion? Today you are going to look at your life in all areas.

If your day-to-day struggle is trying to track the success of your stocks and bonds, then *Stand Up!* is NOT for you. If your day-to-day struggle is working to obtain money to pay the bills and figuring out if you will have enough left over to feed your family, then *Stand Up!* is for you. If you are living paycheck to paycheck or don't even see a paycheck, then *Stand Up!* is for you. If you are stuck in the same routine day-after-day and need a change, then *Stand Up!* is for you. If you're struggling with addictions or abuse, then *Stand Up!* is for you. If you are sick and tired of being sick and tired, then *Stand Up!* is for you.

Remember:

> *Just because it's the life you know doesn't mean it's the way to go.*

Stand Up! For Yourself is designed to help you *Step Toward a New Direction Using Principles!* This is not a book for leisure reading. In fact, for some, it is a must read. It is not a book that you put down and say, "Oh, that was nice." *Stand Up!* is intended to cause you to take action.

You are going to take a hard look at your current situation by completing the *Stand Up! Quality Living Continuum* and discovering your current pathway. You are going to identify your *purpose and vision*. You are going to examine your *faith,* and then you are going to be *determined* to *Stand Up!* by getting it *together, working cooperatively* and *responsibly*, showing *a loving attitude*, learning to be *resourceful*, and *disciplining* your actions to improve your overall wellbeing so you can prosper and have quality living.

Now, you may ask why biblical principles? Why not rules? Standards? Guidelines? The definition of principle, itself, is an affirmation of the intent of *Stand Up!*

- A general *truth* or law.
- A rule of personal *conduct*.
- Collective moral *standards*.
- A criterion for *excellence*.

- An established mode of *action* in natural phenomena.
- One who is well suited to some *purpose* or obviously destined for *success*.
- A person having some remarkable talent, power, or ability.

("Principle" 2019)

Truth! Conduct! Standards! Excellence! Action! Purpose! Success! Ability! All of these action words are at the very core of *Stand Up!*

If I asked you right now, what do you want with your life, I am sure you could give me a long list… perhaps a brand-new home, a new car, a better job, more money in your pocket. Maybe you would say that you want to be healthier, thinner, or that you want to be free from a negative situation that you have going on in your life.

At this exact moment, what if I were to ask you, what do you want *to do* with your life? Adding these action words make all the difference. It puts the responsibility for your life where it needs to be… *with you*! Adding those words gives you direction. It helps you to identify your purpose. If you want to own your own home… then what are YOU going *to do* to make that happen. If you want a better job… what are YOU going *to do* to make that happen? If you want to have the ability to buy whatever you want… then what are YOU going *to do* to make that happen? Do it now, not later! Taking action makes your dreams become your realities. *Stand Up!* is a **do-it-yourself** kit for quality living!

You are at the beginning of a journey to understanding the potential that you hold. Only you can decide what *to do*. It's up to you!

Remember:

>*Nothing happens until you Stand Up! For Yourself and do something.*

LIVING BY THE MOMENTUM

Scripture Ties:

...Be still, and know that I am God...

(Psalm 46:10 NIV)

Now, the next question you need to ask yourself is:

Are you living life by the moment or by the momentum?

If you live life by the moment, then you make every moment count because they are important to you. If you live life by the momentum, you take it as it comes. You go from one tough situation to another tough situation, and it seems as if there are no solutions to your dilemmas. You get so caught up in the day-to-day struggles of "getting by" that you do not take the time to step back and look at the overall picture long enough to change anything. You only look at it long enough to know that you aren't satisfied and that you want something else, something better. Time occurs only in the here and now. The future does not exist except in conversation, "Someday I will…"

In fact, living life by the momentum can become like your favorite old sweater, comfortable to you even if it isn't pretty. You become convinced that this is what life is all about. You feel like this is as good as it gets. But it doesn't have to be that way.

Remember:

> *Go for results, not just activity. Don't settle for less than you deserve.*

There is an African fable of a lion and a gazelle.

> Every morning a gazelle wakes up. It knows it must run faster than the fastest lion or it will be eaten… Every morning a lion wakes up. It knows it must outrun the slowest gazelle or it will starve to death. It doesn't matter whether you are a lion or a gazelle… when the sun comes up, you'd better be running.
>
> (McDougall 2009)

I used to agree with this. I even had a motivational poster of it that hung in my office. But now, I know that is not enough to live to survive. We must live to prosper!

Our challenge is not to run harder. Our challenge is to run differently. There is an African proverb that says, "*To run is not necessarily to arrive*" ("Swahili Wisdom about Patience." 2019). You can't keep doing the exact, same things over and over and expect to get to a better place. It will not happen. What will happen is that you will wake up one day and realize that you have spent the last twenty years doing things that you didn't want to do to stay in a situation that you didn't want to be in. Don't let that be you! Stop running! Stop living a quantity life instead of a quality life—putting in your time but not being able to enjoy your time. It is time for you to *Stand Up! For Yourself and Step Toward a New Direction Using Principles.*

Do you want to survive, or do you want to thrive? I recently read an article about a technique that you can use when you find yourself in deep water. It is called "drownproofing". Drownproofing is floating face down in the water, moving as little as possible and only lifting your head high enough out of the water to take that occasional breath (Kearney 2011). The article made me think of how we often are drownproofing our lives. We wait until we are in deep water, and then we just keep floating along, paralyzed in place, afraid to move, afraid to trouble the waters, only looking up and getting a breath of reality when it is absolutely necessary. We are afraid because of our fear. So, we just stay in deep water and deep water is dark, cold, and scary.

Are you drownproofing? Save yourself! It is time to *Stand Up!* and put your feet on solid ground! Turn it over, and God will teach you to swim or tell you it's not that deep, so just *Stand Up!*

Too many of us live our lives that way. We adapt to a way of life that we do not find acceptable. Do you find yourself just *trying to live instead of living to try*? Are you influencing what happens throughout your day, or are you just going through the motions? When you are living life by the momentum, everything takes a sense of urgency. When you live for the moment you take the time to decide what is important to you. Are you deciding what happens in your life, or do you let your circumstances dictate?

Remember:

> *We are not guaranteed our next moment. Don't take the luxury of giving your moments away. Be sure you are **living a full life and not living life being fooled.***

Do any of the following describe you?

- Try to do as many things as possible in a short amount of time.
- Rush others, impatient, hate to wait.
- High level of stress and anxiety.
- Always struggling with things, with people, with events in your life.

If you answered yes, then you are caught up in the momentum of life. It is time to *Stand Up! For Yourself and Step Toward a New Direction Using Principles.* By applying these principles, you will soon have the confidence and drive to accomplish your goals without the pressures listed above. *Stand Up!* biblical principles are to be applied on a consistent basis to achieve success individually and collectively at work, home, school, church, and in the community.

The nine *Stand Up!* principles are:

- Purpose and Vision
- Faith
- Perseverance
- Togetherness
- Cooperative Work
- Responsibility
- Loving Attitude
- Resourcefulness
- Self-Discipline

While learning about the nine principles, you will also look at your overall wellbeing. You will look at the motivation behind your behaviors, habits, and routines. You will also learn how to set realistic goals for yourself and how to follow through on your action plan for quality living.

Remember:

> *Prosperity will not come to you or meet you halfway; you must step toward it.*

I remember a time in my life when I felt invincible. I felt that I had power, position, and popularity. A friend of mine told me something at that time that I will never forget. She said I was a good leader, but that I had no direction.

She was right. I never moved forward; I only moved in circles. It was only a few years later I found myself back on the same rollercoaster that I had been on since graduating high school: working low-pay jobs, struggling to pay the bills, unable to stay in any type of relationship, cursing my situation in life, arguing with my family, and escaping with my friends to commiserate all of the material things that we didn't have but wanted. I had become accustomed to moving in and out of poverty without arming myself with the necessary tools to stay out of poverty.

So, what about you? Does this sound familiar? Do you find yourself moving in circles also? If you want to shorten the distance from living life by the momentum to living a quality life, then learn from your mistakes and do not continue to repeat them over and over as I have in the past.

Remember:

> *Life is too short to be miserable, so move on and move up!*

Today I am content and right where I want to be in my life. NOT! Quality living is a life-long journey, not a final destination. I recognize that life is filled with ongoing changes. I still experience roadblocks and setbacks. My goals ten years ago are not the same goals I have today. No one has everything perfect in their life, but I know it will never get better if you do not *Stand Up! For Yourself* and use the key to meet any changes that come your way. Realize that you aren't going to find a "drive-thru" solution where all of your problems will be solved in thirty minutes or less. You have to dedicate yourself to the long haul. Don't give up on your goals. Don't give up on your abilities. Don't give up on yourself. Don't give up; it's time to *Stand Up!*

The key to meeting those changes that come your way is—***direction***. I had never thought about what purpose my life holds and what I needed to do to achieve that purpose. You cannot step toward a new direction if you do not know what direction you are going to take. I thought that the only way to have a full life was to fill it. All I learned was that it is possible to look busy, and even be busy while accomplishing nothing. *Stand Up!* will help you, just as it has helped me to look at real-life learning experiences in the quest to find direction.

Today you are going to be honest with yourself and really get a solid look at what is happening in your life. Instead of trying to decide what impact the future is going to have on you, you are going to decide what impact you want to have on your future. And then you are going to set about creating that impact.

Life is like a breakfast of steak and eggs. You can be like the chicken who gave the eggs or the cow who gave the steak! The chicken was involved but easily walked away; however, the cow was definitely committed. Many of us are like the chicken. We are "involved" in our life, we are contributing, but we are not "committed". We are not giving it our all.

Let me say it again, life is too short to be miserable. If you aren't happy, then you need to decide what it is going to take to make you happy and then you need to go for it. I am not talking short-term happiness through temporary methods but long-term happiness through life-changing choices. It's time to stop sleeping with your eyes open. It's time to **Stand Up**, **Stand Out**, and **Stand On** a firm foundation that you are going to build starting today—starting now!

STAND UP! PATHWAYS TO OVERALL WELLBEING

Scripture Ties:

Trust in the Lord with all thine heart; and lean not to thine own understanding. In all thy ways acknowledge him, and he shall direct thy paths.

(Proverbs 3:5–6 KJV)

And my God will meet all your needs according to the riches of his glory in Christ Jesus.

(Philippians 4:19 NIV)

And God is able to bless you abundantly, so that in all things at all times, having all that you need, you will abound in every good work.

(2 Corinthians 9:8 NIV)

Before we start setting our goals, it is important to take a snapshot of where we are at this very moment. When you live life by the momentum, it is very possible that you may be so caught up in your day-to-day activities that you do not even realize that you are at a critical point in one or more of your life areas, which in turn affects your overall wellbeing. Perhaps you are thriving in many areas, so you push the areas of concern further and further back. You tell yourself that you can deal with it later. Then when they become a crisis, they demand all your attention, the areas where you were thriving suddenly begin suffering, and soon you find yourself juggling to make it all work. It is time to break the cycle!

The *Stand Up! Quality Living Continuum* will look at your *overall wellbeing* by looking at twelve control keys in five major life areas to move you from quantity to quality living.

The first life area you will look at is your *personal and interpersonal wellbeing*. This category is about your family and you and focuses on the control keys of everyone's physical and mental health, legal issues, education, and family care. The second major life area is your *material wellbeing,* which is based upon those tangible things that you need to survive: housing, food, transportation, household, and personal necessities. Next, your *financial wellbeing* looks at your resourcefulness as well as how you make your money and how you spend it. Your *social wellbeing* focuses on your relationships with friends, extended family, and your community connections. Are you well connected, or are you living in isolation? And finally, you will examine your *spiritual wellbeing* and look at your connections with your faith community.

By looking at where you are currently in the twelve control keys under the five major life areas for overall wellbeing, you can determine your strengths as well as identify areas where you need to *Stand Up!* The following is a sample of some of the questions that you will ask yourself as you complete the *Stand Up! Quality Living Continuum:*

Life Area One—Personal and Interpersonal Wellbeing Control Keys

Physical and Mental Health:

- Do your family and you participate in routine preventative medical care?

- Do you have routine medical caregivers?
- Do you have affordable, adequate health insurance?

Employment/Education:

- Do your family and you have the jobs that you want?
- The work hours that you want?
- The benefits that you need?

Childcare/Eldercare:

- Do you have quality childcare or eldercare of your choice?

Legal Issues:

- Is anyone in your family dealing with legal issues?

Our Children's Education:

- Are your school-age children succeeding in school?

Life Area Two—Material Wellbeing Control Keys

Housing:

- Do you have housing that you like and can afford?
- Do you own your own home?
- Do you have insurance for your home?

Food:

- Do you have enough food to meet your family's dietary needs?
- Are you able to purchase any food your household desires and eat when and where you want?

Transportation:

- Do you have dependable transportation available?
- Do you have affordable and adequate insurance?

Household and Personal Necessities:

- Are you able to choose and purchase your personal and household supplies that you prefer?

Life Area Three —Financial Wellbeing Control Keys

Money/Budget:

- Do you have permanent employment with enough income and benefits to maintain your household?
- Do you have money set aside for savings and emergencies?

Life Area Four —Social Wellbeing Control Keys

Community Connections:

- Do you have anyone that you can turn to when you need help?
- Is there a language barrier when you are trying to communicate with others?
- Do you know what resources are available to you?

Life Area Five —Spiritual Wellbeing Control Keys

Spiritual:

- Are you able to worship and fellowship with others within your faith community?

The answers to these and the rest of the questions from the *Stand Up! Quality Living Continuum* will then help you to identify which path you are on in each area of your overall wellbeing.

Tom Cochrane wrote the song "Life is a Highway" in the '90s after he took his family to West Africa for a *World Vision Relief* concert. In the song, he talks about life being a road you travel on, one day here and one day gone. *Stand Up!* uses this visualization in the *Stand Up! Quality Living Continuum* by using five pathways to identify your current wellbeing.

If you are on that first or second pathway, then you already know you have hit some tough times. You need to find some roadside assistance. These pathways show danger or potential for danger. These pathways take and keep you in a life of bondage. You are living life by the momentum! You are living a quantity life and not a quality life. You need to be linked with available resources. You do not have to keep struggling. *Stand Up!* can help you find the tools, so you can get off that path, turn around, and move toward a new direction. A direction paved with opportunity.

If you are on the third or fourth pathway, you are stuck. You feel like you are sitting still. You feel like you are spinning your wheels. You are finding roadblocks everywhere you turn. This is a great place to *Stand Up!*, set your goals, and develop your action plan so you can move forward in a positive direction.

If you are on the fifth pathway, you are set on cruise control, you are thriving and enjoying a quality life! We want that for everyone. Perhaps at this point in your journey, you could contribute to the overall wellbeing of others by donating your time or money toward some of the actions listed in the "What's Next" section.

If you are ready, you can access and complete the unabridged *Stand Up! Quality Living Continuum* at the *Stand Up!* website (www.standupinitiative.com) or in the appendix. No matter what path you are on, never just pull over and park. Do not ever give up! Visit the *Stand Up!* website (www.standupinitiative.com) to find resources to move you down the path toward quality living.

I had a dream that I had written about in my *Stand Up!* journal. It was so enlightening to me. I dreamed my family and I were driving up a mountain in a tight single-file formation. I was very anxious and stressed that we were going to run out of gas. I repeatedly had to stop and start because of how closely everyone was following each other. We were moving so slow, and I was so impatient. I couldn't see past the car in front of me. I didn't know where we were going. I just felt I had to keep going with everyone else. My husband kept telling me to turn around so we could get the supplies we needed. I just felt I couldn't. Although there was open road on either side, I just felt there was no way to get out of that line with everyone else. I was afraid, but I didn't know why I was afraid. I resisted and resisted, and my husband persisted and persisted, "Turn around!" Finally, I gave in and when I turned around and went toward a new direction, suddenly, the stress and tension were gone. Out of the blue, the gloominess and clouds were gone, and we were driving into sunshine. My dream was a great example of living life by the momentum and not by the moment.

I was so excited to tell my husband about my dream. He shared with me the following scripture that had come to him while I shared my story.

Enter ye in at the straight gate; for wide is the gate and broad is the way, that leadeth to destruction, and many there be which in thereat; Because straight is the gate, and narrow is the way, which leadeth unto life, and few there be that find it.

(Matthew 7:13–14 KJV)

I felt as if my turnaround had come. I knew I was on a new pathway and that my husband and I were going to fulfill our purpose and help others to *Stand Up!* I want that feeling for you too. I pray that you will turn around if you are going down the wrong path—head into the sunshine!

THE PRINCIPLE OF PURPOSE AND VISION

Scripture Ties:

> For the vision is yet for an appointed time and it hastens to the end [fulfillment]; it will not deceive or disappoint. Though it tarry, wait [earnestly] for it, because it will surely come; it will not be behindhand on its appointed day.
>
> (Habakkuk 2:3 AMPC)

Perhaps earlier, when I asked you who you are, you might have answered in several different ways depending on how you choose to identify yourself. You may have said that you are a parent or instead chose to tell me your occupation. Maybe you identify yourself by where you live, by your age, whom you know, or an event from your past.

The better question to ask would be… do you know *whose you are*? Do you recognize that you are a child of God? Do you recognize God as your father in heaven? Putting Him first will put everything else into perspective and will drive the direction that you will go. Your focus determines your future. Focus on God and let Him drive the vision. Proverbs 19:21 (AMPC) tells us, "Many plans are in a man's mind, but it is the Lord's purpose for him that will stand."

Before you can get started in a new direction, you must first choose that direction by defining your purpose and vision. What are you about? What do you want to do with your life? How do you want to be remembered? What is your purpose, your vision, your mission? No individual or family can become great without a purpose that energizes, inspires, and builds you up.

Only you can identify your purpose and vision. Be sure it really is what you want. Do you think your current situation is your destiny? Your fate? Do you feel you can't change? Don't let your current situation define you. Don't use it as an alibi. Be honest with yourself.

Remember:

> *An effort is not enough without purpose and vision. In other words, don't work so hard toward achieving nothing. We are not guaranteed our next moment. Don't take the luxury of giving your moments away.*

Your purpose and vision will build your morale. Your purpose and vision will reduce frustration and make it easier to make decisions. You can stop focusing on things that will not matter in the long run but consume all of your time now. Your purpose and vision will allow you to concentrate, focus, and prioritize activities in your life. Keep in mind that your purpose and vision should have seven elements:

1. Line up with the word of God.
2. Provide you with direction.
3. Be simple and easily understood.
4. Be something you enjoy.
5. Be something you can achieve.

6. Be something you can see yourself doing long term.

7. It should answer the question—What are you about?

Your purpose and vision must be something you believe in and can carry with you always. Effort and courage will never be enough without purpose and vision.

My personal purpose and vision are to help others. I attempt to do this through the career that I have chosen through my life with my family and, most importantly, through my relationship with God. It is in line with the word, it provides me with direction, it's simple and easily understood, it is something I enjoy, it is something that I can achieve, and it defines me and tells everyone what I am about. It also has vision and is something I can see myself doing long term.

> To everything there is a season, and a time to every purpose under heaven.
>
> (Ecclesiastes 3:1 KJV)

It is your season! Now is the time for you to identify your purpose and vision. Proclaim it! Say it to yourself right now to confirm it, share it with someone you trust, write it down here. Read it! Believe it! Say it! Receive it!

Also, share it on the *Stand Up!* website (www.standupinitiative.com). This will make it real to you and provide you with a constant reminder.

Remember:

> *Your words, dreams, and thoughts have power to create the condition of your life. Let it be the life you want! What you talk about, what you dream about, what you think about, you can bring about!*

My Purpose and Vision:

_____

_____

_____

_____

_____

_____

THE PRINCIPLE OF FAITH

Scripture Ties:

And without faith it is impossible to please him, for whoever would draw near to God must believe that he exists and that he rewards those who seek him.

(Hebrews 11:6 ESV)

Hebrews 11:1 (KJV) says, "Now faith is the substance of things hoped for, the evidence of things not seen." Faith has movement and will give you the courage to *Stand Up!* and step toward that new direction. Faith will remove all limits. All things are possible with faith. By identifying your purpose, your view of everything will change. Instead of focusing on the bottom line, you are going to focus on the horizon and what is ahead.

There is a saying, "Sorrow looks back, worry looks around, and faith looks up" ("Quote by Ralph Waldo Emerson" 2019). If you visualize that saying and see yourself as someone who is always feeling sorry and worrying about things, then you find yourself shaking your head no! Because you are always looking back and looking around, you are always being negative. BUT if you focus on hope and faith, you see yourself looking ahead and looking up, and you find yourself nodding yes! And soon you are moving forward in your life instead of going in circles in your life. I've always said, *If you worry, you aren't praying, and if you're praying, don't worry!* The Bible tells us, "Who of you by worrying can add a single hour to his life?" (Matthew 6:25 NIV).

Faith requires positive expectations. Faith gives us the power to overcome the trials and tribulations that we face. People with faith are characterized as brave, calm, confident, collected, cool, fearless, happy, hopeful, secure, and sure of themselves. Do those words describe you? Or do you identify with the following? Anxiety, depression, doubt, fear, hopelessness, insecurity, lack of confidence, shyness, uncertainty, unhappiness, and worry. If these describe you, then you must build your faith. A lack of faith can keep you in a self-destructive pattern of behavior. A lack of faith can keep you living by the momentum. A lack of faith will keep you drownproofing! It is time to *Stand Up!* and find a purpose and vision in which you can have faith. This will be very important on your journey toward a new direction.

Faith is the catalyst that will lead you down the road toward your purpose. Quit questioning why negative things are happening and instead question how you can use them to make positive things happen in your life and the lives of others. Faith is embodied in hope. Faith sees the impossible and accepts the incredible.

My dad always told me that when I am feeling hopeless about a situation to remember that there is always someone out there who is worse off than I am and I should be thankful for the blessings I have been given. There is a saying, "There, but for the grace of God, go I" ("Quote by John Bradford" 2019). Remember to count your blessings even in the storms.

I actually keep a running list of things for which I am thankful. Anytime something positive happens, I add it to the list and when I am down or going through a trial or tribulation, I pull out my list and remember that I have so much to be thankful for. Share your blessings *In The Storm* story on the *Stand Up!* website (www.standupinitiative.com).

Remember:

> *It's the rough days that make us appreciate the good days. Don't take any of your days for granted.*

So, now it is time to ask yourself:

- Do you recognize your faith?
- Does that faith give you confidence in yourself and your abilities?
- Does that faith give you confidence in the events and activities that you deal with daily?
- Does that faith give you confidence in the people you interact with daily?
- Are you in a spiritual stupor?

Wake Up! And *Stand Up!* You must find your faith and conviction before you can step toward a new direction. Use your faith to enrich your family, community, and yourself. Faith will help you deal with and overcome the obstacles and roadblocks that you will encounter along the way.

Remember:

Don't "think" you can, "know" you can! Believe it, and you will achieve it—deceive it, and you will grieve it.

THE PRINCIPLE OF PERSEVERANCE

Scripture Ties:

I don't mean to say that I have already achieved these things or that I have already reached perfection. But I press on to possess that perfection for which Christ Jesus first possessed me."

(Philippian 3:12 NLT)

For everything that was written in the past was written to teach us, so that through the endurance taught in the Scriptures and the encouragement they provide we might have hope.

(Romans 15:4 NIV)

Remember:

There is no such thing as missed opportunities only ignored opportunities.

There are people who think about what to do and those who go out and do it. We all get into our comfort zones. I have always said, *It is easier to deal with a familiar pain than to deal with change.* Many of us postpone what matters to us because it doesn't seem obtainable. We often limit our vision. It becomes easy to wrap excuses around our lives.

To me, the opposite of perseverance is procrastination. Do not put off what needs to be done. It isn't going to go away. It is just going to become a bigger issue.

Remember:

> *Put out your fires before they turn into flames. Things may seem too big to tackle, but nothing is insurmountable. You just have to Stand Up! and step toward a new direction.*

I tell you the truth, you can say to this mountain, 'May you be lifted up and thrown into the sea,' and it will happen. But you must really believe it will happen and have no doubt in your heart.

(Mark 11:23 NLT)

Without direction, perseverance becomes indifference and disappointment. Stating your purpose and vision points you in the right direction, having faith causes you to take the first step, but it is perseverance that will keep you moving down the right road.

Right now, write down the first thing that pops into your mind when you read the first few words of each sentence below.

- I have to _____
- I ought to _____
- I should _____
- I can't _____
- I must _____
- I really couldn't _____
- I am not able to _____

Now cross off the beginnings of those sentences and replace them with "I want" and "I choose to". Do you limit yourself because of what you think you have to do or what you think you can't do? Realize that every obstacle presents an opportunity to improve your situation.

Take a puzzle and turn all the pieces face down. Try to put the puzzle together. Not that easy, right? Once the blank puzzle is together, write your purpose and vision across it and see how much quicker it all comes together. Is that how you are tackling life? Are you trying to make the pieces fit without looking at the overall picture? Are you making it more difficult than it has to be? Do you feel you have no choice but to accept things the way they are? You do have a choice! Be determined in your purpose and see yourself achieving it.

My *Stand Up!* journey began over twenty years ago when I first decided to commit the program to paper. I remembered I was so excited when it was finished. I remembered the saying, "If you build it, they will come" ("Quote from Field of Dreams" 2019). I sent out flyers to several agencies and spent money renting out a meeting room and buying refreshments. Absolutely, no one came! I was so embarrassed and discouraged, but I did not quit. I kept writing and reworking it and eventually began presenting it at various seminars and conferences. Although it was successful, I knew it was not reaching the audience for which it was written. So, I stopped and prayed for God to give me direction. I even had to put it on the shelf for a period of time as I dealt with several life events. However, I knew that it is my purpose to help people through this book, so I persevered. I hope that it will help you! If you have a vision, never give up! *Stand Up!* and step toward a new direction.

My mom taught me a saying when I was young that I have passed on to my children and grandchildren. "Good, better, best, never let it rest until your good is better and your better is best" ("Quote by St. Jerome" 2019). "Don't let others tell you what you can't do!" ("Quote by Roy T. Bennett:" 2019). Instead, show them what you can do! Be a *find-a-way-make-a-way* person! You deserve to have the chance to open your wings and soar to your highest heights!

Remember:

> *Don't accept the unacceptable. Keep on, keeping on! Don't be afraid to Stand Up! For Yourself and Step Toward a New Direction Using the Principles that you are learning.*

How many of you have prevented yourself from any of the following because you felt you didn't deserve it? Determine today that you will no longer permit yourself to feel undeserving of what is rightfully yours!

1. Right to equality
2. Freedom from discrimination
3. Right to life, liberty, personal security
4. Freedom from slavery
5. Freedom from torture and degrading treatment
6. Right to Recognition as a person before the law
7. Right to equality before the law
8. Freedom from arbitrary arrest and exile
9. Right to fair public hearing
10. Right to be considered innocent until proven guilty
11. Freedom from interference with privacy, family, home and correspondence
12. Right to free movement in and out of the country
13. Right to asylum in other countries from persecution
14. Right to a nationality and the freedom to change it
15. Right to marriage and family
16. Right to own property
17. Freedom of belief and religion

18. Freedom of opinion and information
19. Right of peaceful assembly and association
20. Right to participate in government and in free elections
21. Right to social security
22. Right to desirable work
23. Right to rest and leisure
24. Right to adequate living standards
25. Right to education
26. Right to participate in the cultural life of community
27. Right to a social order
28. Community duties essential to free and full development
29. Freedom from State or personal interference in the above rights

(Adapted from "Universal Declaration of Human Rights" n.d.)

Perseverance through hardship.

("Adinkra Symbols of West Africa" 2007a)

THE PRINCIPLE OF TOGETHERNESS

Scripture Ties:

Again I say to you, if two of you agree on earth about anything they ask, it will be done for them by my Father in heaven. For where two or three are gathered in my name, there am I among them.

(Matthew 18:19–20 ESV)

As we have therefore opportunity, let us do good unto all men, especially unto them who are of the household of faith.

(Galatians 6:10 KJV)

And if one prevail against him, two shall withstand him, and a threefold cord is not quickly broken.

(Ecclesiastes 4:12 KJV)

It is true that it takes perseverance. However, it makes it a lot easier if we have support. Everyone wants to belong. I love the definition of the word "belong":

> Be^long, v. 1: to feel and be a part of… i.e. Of a community, a workplace, a church, a neighborhood or school 2: to enjoy a sense of contribution, value, self-worth 3: to truly believe one is a natural and equal part of the whole 4: comfortable, safe, cared for, welcome.
>
> ("Diversity Shirts" 2019)

Why "togetherness" as a principle instead of teamwork, partnership, or collaboration? It is because you, personally, have to get yourself "together" before you can hope to find success together with others! Even the catchphrase for T.E.A.M. (Together Everyone Achieves More) begins with the word "together". Whether a family, team, or workgroup is effective depends on how "together" they are in their purpose and vision. When individual's strengths are interwoven, the chance for success of the purpose and vision is magnified.

Coming together is a start; *staying* together shows progress; *working* together leads to results! (Paraphrased "Quote by Edward Everett Hale" 2019). Think about someone who is important to you in your life. Then think of the things that you have in common with the person and things that show that you are totally different from this person. Realize it is our similarities that join us together and our differences that enhance and broaden our lives.

Have you ever seen the following riddle?

- Put together this chain so that it is as strong as possible.
- Use the following links: two 100-pound links, two 50-pound links, and one 25-pound link.

How can we arrange the links for maximum strength and effectiveness? The truth is it doesn't matter. A chain is only as strong as its weakest link. We need to *Stand Up!* with each other. We need to be strong together! "He brought them out of darkness, the utter darkness, and broke away their chains" (Psalm 107:14 NIV). *Stand Up!* together with God leading the way.

There is an African proverb that says, "Sticks in a bundle are unbreakable" ("Kenyan Proverb" n.d.). If we are to succeed, we need to surround ourselves with those that have a common cause, a similar purpose and vision, and a clear direction. If you are determined to *Stand Up!* for yourself and others are not ready for this, you need to share *Stand Up!* with them and bring them on board or consider that relationship.

I can remember when I lived in a housing project in Texas, the neighbor man and I would talk frequently. He fought with drug addiction for years. He had not worked in a long time and was waiting on an insurance settlement from a car accident. He would tell me every day how he was going to use some of that settlement money for a down payment on a house and how he was going to use the rest to start a little restaurant. He dreamed about it daily. He drew it on paper and would show me the layout of the restaurant and what name he had chosen and whom he wanted to work there. He quit going out so much at night and started going to church.

I knew his money must have finally come when I saw a steady stream of men and women going into his house. He managed to smoke and drink away all of his proceeds in one week. People came out of nowhere when they heard that he had money. They knew his weakness, and they preyed upon him. They say misery loves company. It is easy to continue making poor choices if you are surrounded by others who are making poor choices.

Take responsibility for your decisions. You cannot force others to see your vision, but you can discipline yourself so that you do not give in to the pressures of others. When people see you *Stand Up! For yourself* and make changes, they may become critical of your new aspirations and plans. They are familiar with the old you. If you worry about what they think, they can become an alibi keeping you from your goals.

It doesn't mean that you have to abandon your old friends or stop talking to your family. Tell them what you are trying to achieve, and when they see you living a quality life, they will come around sooner or later to *Stand Up!* with you. They say you can't teach an old dog new tricks, but I say to the old dogs, quit teaching your old tricks to the new dogs! No one will ever get ahead that way!

Remember:

> *John 10:10 (NLT) tells us that "The thief's purpose is to steal and kill and destroy. My purpose is to give them a rich and satisfying life." Don't waste time on people who are time wasters!*

You know the type, the ones who are always blowing small aggravations out of proportion, trying to convince you to do negative actions, dwelling in the past, worrying about stuff that may never happen or worrying about what others are doing or what others have. Surround yourself with those who can go the distance with you. This is where your faith and surrounding yourself with like-minded people will keep you strong.

Show me your friends, I'll show you your future.

("Quote by Moosa Rahat" 2019)

Take a minute to review your communication circles. Draw a circle inside a circle and inside another circle. You are represented in the middle circle. In the second circle, write the names of the people that you feel you should maintain good lines of communication on a daily basis and list why you feel it is important.

In the third circle, write the names of the people that you feel you should communicate with no less than weekly. And outside of the circles write down the people you feel you should maintain good lines of communication on a less frequent basis.

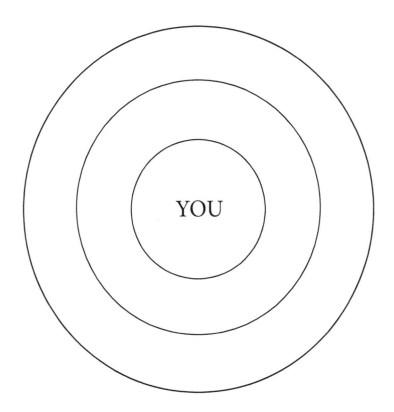

In reviewing your circles,

- Are they an accurate representation of your current lines of communication?

- Are there changes that you see you want to make?

Recognize that these people are your network of support to achieve your purpose.

- Are you surrounding yourself with positive people?
- Are your lines of communication open?
- Does the person that cashes your checks know more about your family finances than your family?
- Do your co-workers know your goals better than your family?
- Do your friends know your plans better than your spouse?

Work toward togetherness with those who are most important to you, have a similar purpose and vision as yours, and want to *Stand Up!* for themselves too. If you have children, you need to bring them on board with your way of thinking. When you are living life by the momentum, you can often find that everyone in the house is running on their own track doing their own thing. If you are going to live by the moment you need to get your entire family to see the purpose and vision that you see. In my family, I'm not just one person, I am twenty people strong.

There are trees in California that grow "300 feet tall and live for hundreds of years. For all their magnificence, one would believe that they require a deep root system to keep them upright. Instead, they have roots that spread out along the surface of the forest floor to capture all the moisture possible, intertwining with the roots of other trees in the grove. The interlocking roots securely support and sustain these giant trees when the storms strike and fierce winds blow. The trees' survival depends on the combined support of one another" ("Jefferson Ruritan Club" 2016)one would think the redwoods would require a deep root system to keep them upright. Instead, they have roots that spread out along the surface of the forest floor to capture all the moisture possible, intertwining with the roots of other redwoods in the grove. The interlocking roots securely support and sustain these giant sequoias when storms strike and fierce winds blow. The trees' survival depends on the combined support of one another. When we stand together.....support one another.....encourage one another..... we become stronger together, and like the giant redwoods, we keep growing taller. The great redwoods message reminds us that our strength is in our support of each other.

"When we stand together… support one another… encourage one another… we become strong together… and like those giant trees we" are then able to *Stand Up!*, stand strong, and continue to grow! ("Jefferson Ruritan Club" 2016) one would think the redwoods would require a deep root system to keep them upright. Instead, they have roots that spread out along the surface of the forest floor to capture all the moisture possible, intertwining with the roots of other redwoods in the grove. The interlocking roots securely support and sustain these giant sequoias when storms strike and fierce winds blow. The trees' survival depends on the combined support of one another. When we stand together…..support one another…..encourage one another…..we become stronger together, and like the giant redwoods, we keep growing taller. The great redwoods message reminds us that our strength is in our support of each other. It is time for you to take root and branch out. Starting a *Stand Up! Life Group* is an excellent way to surround yourself with others of similar purpose and vision. Visit the *Stand Up!* website (www.standupinitiative.com) for additional ideas or to leave your suggestions and successes!

Unity is Strength.

("Ganda (Uganda) Proverb" n.d.)

THE PRINCIPLE OF COOPERATIVE WORK

Spiritual Ties:

> So we built the wall. And all the wall was joined together to half its height, for the people had a mind to work.
>
> (Nehemiah 4:6 ESV)

> Do two walk together, unless they have agreed to meet?
>
> (Amos 3:3 ESV)

> Behold, how good and pleasant it is when brothers dwell in unity!
>
> (Psalms 133:1 ESV)

Have you ever read the following?

This is a story about four people named EVERYBODY, SOMEBODY, ANYBODY, and NOBODY. There was an important job to do and EVERYBODY was asked to do it. EVERYBODY was sure SOMEBODY would do it. SOMEBODY would do it if ANYBODY would help. ANYBODY could have done it, but NOBODY wanted to. SOMEBODY became angry because it was EVERYBODY's job, but NOBODY realized that EVERYBODY wouldn't do it. It ended up that EVERYBODY blamed SOMEBODY when NOBODY did what ANYBODY could have done.

("Inspirational and Motivational Quotes: Anonymous Simplified Version of 'A Poem About Responsibility' by Charles Osgood." 2019)

It takes cooperation to make everything work in your life. Without it, you have chaos and crisis. Working together cooperatively leads to coordination of effort, productivity, good communication, and other positive benefits. There is a Chinese proverb that says, "Behind an able man there are always other able men" ("Chinese Proverb" n.d.). Don't feel that you are the only one that can get things done. Share your burdens.

One of my co-workers at a former job was an elderly single mother of two grown sons. The youngest son had just moved, and she found herself alone for the first time in her life. She shared that she remembers when the boys were growing up, she felt it was important to keep the house in top order. She wanted everything done in a particular way and didn't want anyone to help because it seemed that no one ever did it right.

She said in retrospect, "Who cares how clean my floors were twenty years ago and whether there were cobwebs on my ceiling. I wish I would have worried less about the house and spent more time with the kids."

I, personally, am definitely not a "Suzy Homemaker". This is not and never will be an area of strength for me—just ask my husband. I call our cobwebs fancy doilies and tell everyone that dust is actually a protective covering for furniture.

Now my mother, on the other hand, was a superwoman to me. I love the stories that my parents, aunts, and uncles tell about their childhood. I also have fond memories of my childhood with my siblings and cousins. In the past, there was more interaction with people. We have moved from a "hands-on-do-it-yourself" society to a "push-button" society to a "voice-activated" society to a "virtual reality" society. People today do everything from their seat and not on their feet. Instead of playing games outdoors, you see children sitting alone using cell phones and devices. Often no one even looks up when talking.

Take a second and write down your daily interactions with your family members. And I am talking true interactions with actual eye-to-eye and knee-to-knee ICU (I see you) communication. Is your list long or short? Are you struggling to think of things that you do together regularly?

I remember that my mother use to have a three-course meal on the table every evening when my father came home from work. She kept the house immaculate. The only chore my siblings and I were asked to do was to keep our rooms straightened, and usually, she would do that if we conveniently forgot.

Unfortunately, I learned that spoiled is not necessarily good unless you can figure out how to be spoiled all of your life. Another word for spoiled is rotten, and we don't want our children to be rotten. That is why it is important to *Stand Up!* and step toward a new direction at home too! Tell your family that it is going to take all of you to get ahead. Have each of them participate in this journey with you. They all need to live these principles.

Give each of your family members daily tasks to complete and spend planned, critical "ICU" time together. Some of these tasks will be specific to them, such as making their bed or putting away their clothes. Some of these tasks can be rotated, such as taking out the trash or helping with the dishes. Let your family know your expectations so that they can be self-sufficient when they are older. Balance that with an equal portion of love and affection so that as they leave home, they and you have wonderful memories of their childhood and so you feel you have equipped them with the skills they need to be successful adults.

> And let us consider how to stir up one another to love and good works, not neglecting to meet together, as is the habit of some, but encouraging one another, and all the more as you see the Day drawing near.
>
> (Hebrews 10:24–25 ESV)

In today's society, it is possible to get so caught up in the momentum of life that you may not even have time to see those in your own household. Do what this scripture advises, spend some time each evening talking about the events of the day and encouraging each other. A great time to do this is around the dinner table with everyone's cell phones and devices put away. Schedule other critical "ICU" activities, such as family Bible study, date night, or game night.

In order to encourage cooperation, develop expectations for your family and write down the rules. Discuss what happens when everyone meets the expectations and the consequences when someone breaks the rules. Here is a list that you can use, but feel free to take it and add things that will work for you in your situations:

1. Have written rules and expectations and review them often.

2. Be consistent with your expectations.

3. Follow through with consequences.

4. Reminders are ok as needed but do not assume responsibility that belongs to someone else.

5. Give directions in steps. Give one or two steps to be completed first, then move on until the job is completed. Write the steps down if this proves helpful.

6. When someone is doing something for the first time, do it with them or even more times if necessary until they have confidence in completing the task themselves.

7. Have them repeat the directions back, so you know that they heard the directions correctly.

8. Limit the number of distractions, if possible.

9. Maintain eye contact when giving instructions.

10. Be quick to praise.

11. Explain the reasons behind your instructions.

12. When giving options and instructions, make sure

that they have all the information necessary for them to make good choices.

13. Remember to speak with and show respect, and expect it in return.

14. Be aware of your volume and tone; sometimes it is not so much what you say as to how you say it. Don't yell. Keep the attitude out of your voice.

15. If it isn't the way you would speak to your boss or pastor, then it shouldn't be a way you speak to your family.

16. Check out the finished product.

Remember:

You have to inspect what you expect!

The *Stand Up!* website (www.standupinitiative.com) has a "Household Responsibility and ICU Checklist" that you and your family can complete so that you can see everyone's progress.

THE PRINCIPLE OF RESPONSIBILITY

Scripture Ties:

But if anyone does not provide for his relatives, and especially for members of his household, he has denied the faith and is worse than an unbeliever.

(1 Timothy 5:8 ESV)

And he answered, 'You shall love the Lord your God with all your heart and with all your soul and with all your strength and with all your mind, and your neighbor as yourself.'

(Luke 10:27 ESV)

Be devoted to one another in brotherly love; give preference to one another in honor.

(Romans 12:10 NASB)

> Do nothing from selfishness or empty conceit, but with humility of mind let each of you regard one another as more important than himself.
>
> (Philippians 2:3 NASB)

The following is a difficult word for many people—responsibility. Let's take the two words that you hear in the word responsibility and show it in the following formula:

RESPONSE + ABILITY = Our *ability* to *respond* appropriately in a situation.

Our view of our degree of responsibility is directly related to our *DNA match* to a situation. Just as each of us is made from our distinctive genetic chromosomes, we also have our own distinctive responses to situations that the acronym, DNA, can be used for, such as…

- "**D**" stands for *Devotion* and *Dedication*. It is our commitment to one another or a situation. What are we willing to do to get our desired results?

- **"N"** stands for *Need to Negotiate* when *Necessary.* This is our willingness to compromise, to give and take. This is our ability to communicate. In any situation, it is our human nature to first think, "What's in this for me?" How many of us shut down when things do not go our way? How many of us get angry when we feel we have been left out of a communication circle?

- **"A"** stands for *Acceptance.* This is our acceptance of one another or the situation.

If I am not *devoted* to *Stand Up!* and willing to *negotiate* compromise when something is revealed that I need to change and in *acceptance* of the expectations and consequences of my actions, then I may not feel a strong level of responsibility.

Just as DNA spirals upwards with strand upon strand built on top of one another, such is responsibility. There is a system of cause and effect. It may be your responsibility to take care of your family that causes your commitment to your job. It may be your responsibility to yourself that causes you to exercise and eat right.

We need to recognize three levels of responsibility toward our Overall Wellbeing:

- Responsibility for oneself, both physically, mentally, and spiritually.
- Responsibility for our relationships with others.
- Responsibility for our role in society.

In regards to *responsibility for oneself,* how well do you take care of yourself physically, mentally, and spiritually? If you don't like something about yourself, fix it or forget about it! Realize that sometimes you can be your own worst enemy.

> Do you not know that your bodies are temples of the Holy Spirit, who is in you, whom you have received from God? You are not your own; you were bought at a price. Therefore honor God with your bodies.
>
> (1 Corinthians 6:19–20 NIV)

Answer the following true or false questions to determine if you have strong personal habits or if this is an area that you need to address.

Stand Up! Health Awareness Appraisal

1. I participate in activities of spiritual growth daily.

2. I participate in some type of physical activity daily (walking, active work, sporting activities).

3. I do not spend more than two social hours daily on electronic devices.

4. I eat a wide variety of healthy food.

5. I do not drink alcoholic beverages excessively (0–7 per week).

6. I do not take non-prescribed drugs or prescription drugs improperly.

7. I do not use tobacco or vaping products.

8. I practice safe sexual practices.

9. I seldom experience depression or anxiety.

10. I have routine dental and physical exams to ensure good health.

If you answered "True" to nine out of ten questions, then you have a commendable lifestyle based on sensible habits and a strong awareness of the importance of making good lifestyle choices. Keep it up!

If you answered "True" to seven out of ten questions, then although your lifestyle choices are acceptable you may want to consider some minor change.

If you answered "True" to six out of ten questions, then you are taking unnecessary risks with your health. Several of your habits should be changed if potential health problems are to be avoided. This would be a great goal area for you to establish.

If you answered "True" to five or less questions, then you are making hazardous lifestyle choices. Either you have little personal awareness of good health habits, or you are choosing to ignore them. This is a danger zone. It is critical that you get help. Visit the *Stand Up!* website (www.standupinitiative.com) for available resources.

Next, we need to look at our responsibility for our relationship with others. "*What you speak about, you bring about*" (Zimmerman 2016). If you are always talking negative, then negativity will find you. Proverbs 18:21 (KJV) tells us, "Death and life are in the power of the tongue…" I have the following quote in my office:

> I Am the Decisive Element
>
> I've come to the frightening conclusion that I am the decisive element in a person's life. It's my personal approach that creates the climate; it's my daily mood that makes the weather. I possess tremendous power to make a person's life miserable or joyous. I can be a tool of torture or an instrument of inspiration; I can humiliate or humor, hurt or heal. In all situations, it is my response that decides whether a crisis will be escalated or de-escalated and a person humanized or de-humanized.
>
> ("Quote by Haim G. Ginott" 2019)

That is very powerful. We can bless or curse, encourage or discourage, inspire or instigate, do or undo, make or take, harm, or heal. How do you treat those you come in contact with daily? Do they look forward to talking to you or find a reason to avoid you? God reminds us that, "Everyone should be quick to listen, slow to speak and slow to become angry because human anger does not produce the righteousness that God desires" (James 1:19–20 NIV). Our communication style is unique. None of us talk exactly the same way. Your style reveals your character to everyone else. Your attitude, beliefs, perceptions, the quality of your thinking, and your values are all conveyed in your communication style. Realize that once you say it, you cannot reverse it. Do you recognize any of these negative communication types?

- The Bully—harsh, tough, intimidating.
- Megaphone—talks a lot and very loudly.
- Bubble Buster—never has anything positive to say.
- Space Cadet—always speaking off-topic.
- Clam—chooses to give the silent treatment.
- Nitpicker—always critical.
- Cry Baby—always whining and pouting.
- Backstabber—talks negatively about others.

We need to think more than we talk, talk less than we listen, and think more than we listen or talk! In regards to our responsibility for others, communication plays a key. Not only is it important to be aware of how we speak to others, but we also need to be good listeners. There is a joke that says that the opposite of speaking is waiting to speak. We need to practice good listening skills when interacting with others. We need to be sure that we do not step on other's words. Are you someone who speaks "to" others, or do you speak "at" others?

Remember:

> *Encourage, don't discourage! We need to be non-judgmental in our listening. It is important that we understand the message that is being given.*

Listening is not a subject we study in school. We have to practice listening on our own. Advances in technology make it even more complex as we try to communicate in new ways. It can be difficult to listen for someone's true message when we are getting so much of our daily communication not only by word of mouth but through texts and social media. Listen with your heart. Listening is not necessarily agreeing with the message but respecting the messenger enough to give your undivided attention.

You never really understand a person until you consider things from their point of view. Understanding how someone else feels by putting yourself in his or her place is the starting place of caring and compassion. True compassion means showing you care by doing something. Take action! If a friend is in trouble, don't just feel bad for them, do something about it. Get into the habit of not only praying for others but also standing with others. Compassion is often returned to you after you've given it to other people first.

Finally, we have a responsibility for our role in society. Earlier, we talked about our basic human rights. We need to realize that with every right comes a corresponding responsibility. What does the world need from you? *We can depend on people, or we can lead people.* In order to *Stand Up!* you first have to grow up! 1 Corinthians 13:11 (KJV) tells us,

> When I was a child, I spake as a child, I understood as a child, I thought as a child: but when I became a man, I put away childish things.

Think about how children behave. They like to play all day, they don't have any responsibilities, they pout when they don't get their way, they get jealous of what another child has, they want to be the center of attention, they tattle on others, they quarrel over every little thing, they don't care whom they embarrass, they have short attention spans, they can be very wasteful, they can be rude, they want what they want when they want it, and they don't like to hear the word "no," but they like to say it.

If you identified with a lot of the things on this list, then before you can *Stand Up!* you need to grow up! Don't be a troublemaker, be a troubleshooter! Leave those negative childhood behaviors behind and focus on the positive ones. Children have unending energy, a terrific imagination of unlimited possibilities, they get over things quickly, and they have faith that everything is going to be all right. These are the traits we can use as we *Stand Up!* and step toward a new direction.

When we are living life by the momentum, we are often not even aware of what is going on beyond our own personal world. I want to tell you about a particular breed of the Japanese Koi fish that has amazing growth potential. When placed in a fishbowl, this fish will stay small. It will only grow two or three inches in length. If you take that same fish and move it to a tank, it will grow to the size of the tank six to ten inches. If you take that same fish and throw it into a pond it can grow up to three feet long. The size of the fish is directly related to the size of its world.

What is the size of your world? Are you growing? Or do you feel confined by your environment? How aware are you of things in your world? In order to step toward your role in society, you need to play an active part. This cannot happen if you never leave the block where you live. This cannot happen if you keep living life on the momentum rollercoaster.

Some positive actions you can take in this area are to simply begin watching the news to raise your awareness of world events. Ask your family to watch also and discuss what you see and hear. Pray for our country and our leaders. Watch motivational, as well as informative programs and discuss these with your family and friends. Talk to someone new at work. Join a faith community or civic group. Step out of your comfort zone and greet at least one new person each week. Volunteer at a public service agency or in a faith community. Also, encourage your family to volunteer. Venture outside of your neighborhood. Share the *Stand*

Up! Quality Living Continuum with others through community outreach. Start a *Stand Up! Life Group*. The possibilities to make a difference in your world are endless!

Remember:

> *We spread a way of life, whenever we act.* Be sure to go to the Stand Up! website (www.standup-initiative.com) and tell us how you are making a difference.

Help me and let me help you.

("Adinkra Symbols of West Africa" 2007b)

THE PRINCIPLE OF A LOVING ATTITUDE

Scripture Ties:

Whereas the object *and* purpose of our instruction *and* charge is love, which springs from a pure heart and a good (clear) conscience and sincere (unfeigned)faith.

(1 Timothy 1:5 AMPC)

Love one another with brotherly affection [as members of one family], giving precedence and showing honor to one another.

(Romans 12:10 AMPC)

Little children, let us not love [merely] in theory or in speech but in deed and in truth (in practice and in sincerity).

(1 John 3:18 AMPC)

Love does no wrong to one's neighbor [it never hurts anybody]. Therefore love meets all the requirements *and* is the fulfilling of the Law.

(Romans 13:10 AMPC)

Love bears up under anything *and* everything that comes, is ever ready to believe the best of every person, its hopes are fadeless under all circumstances, and it endures everything [without weakening].

(1 Corinthians 13:7 AMPC)

Love seems to be a hard word for some people, yet it is used in the Bible more than 300 times. We cannot function well without love and respect for one another. My dad's purpose statement is known by anyone that meets him. He ends his conversations with it. He wears it on a pin on his shirt every day, and he has it hanging up in his house. My dad's purpose and vision are to let as many people know as possible that "all we need to do is love one another". It is such a beautiful sentiment, yet so hard to achieve. I think one of the reasons that it is so hard to achieve is that we don't take the time to raise our level of awareness about ourselves and about one another. We need to have an attitude of gratitude.

In the Bible, we learn of the beatitudes in Matthew and Luke that focus on a spirit of love and humility of mercy and compassion. What is your attitude? Your attitude affects the way you relate to others. Does your attitude show love and respect? When attitudes are extreme they can be detrimental to relationships. Can you identify with any of the following attitudes?

1. *Emotional Attitude* —People who react emotionally make comments such as "Why don't they…" Why do I have to…" "I wish someone would…" An emotional attitude may be described as having a mistrust of others. The fear and distrust, the dislike and anger may be so continually expressed that it affects others around them. "A man without self-control is as defenseless as a city with broken-down walls" (Proverbs 25:28 TLB).

2. *Promising Attitude* —People who use a promising attitude may buy time for dealing with a short-term situation but can quickly lose their credibility if the promise is not grounded in truth. It is important to be a man or woman of your word.

Don't tell someone it isn't going to hurt if it is. Be sure you are making promises that you can keep so that those who interact with you will not develop mistrust. "Those who guard their mouths and their tongues keep themselves from calamity" (Proverbs 13:3 NIV).

3. *Controlling Attitude* —People who use a controlling attitude tend to threaten and command instead of making requests of others. A controlling attitude may get results, but the results will not last as those who interact with people who have controlling attitudes look for ways to escape quickly. "If you are sensible, you will control your temper. When someone wrongs you, it is a great virtue to ignore it" (Proverbs 19:11 GNT).

4. *Giving Attitude* —These individuals can overindulge and drain themselves quickly. They often will feel taken advantage of when individuals they interact with demand more and more. A person with a giving attitude can end up feeling resentful to-

ward others. "The wise man saves for the future, but the foolish man spends whatever he gets" (Proverbs 21:20 TLB).

If *attitude* is an area where you struggle, then be sure to identify it as a goal and track your progress. Practice self-control by taking a deep breath before responding to anything. Say it in your head before you let it come out of your mouth.

Realize that your attitude holds power. It is your attitude that can make someone's life miserable or joyous. Your attitude can be used to be cruel or to be kind. Your attitude can hurt or heal a situation. However, it is a *Loving Attitude* which meets the requirements of every situation. It is firm but fair.

> 5. *Loving Attitude* —People who are truthful and trustworthy with others. It is passionate and shows empathy, concern, and caring for others. It is long-standing and shows tolerance and acceptance of others. People with a loving attitude master their moods. They live by their commitments, not their emotions. These people do the right thing even when they don't feel like it. People with a loving at-

titude watch their words. They know there is power in the tongue. They put their minds to work before opening their mouths. People with a loving attitude restrain their reactions. They can control their temper and do not keep track of wrongs. People with a loving attitude maintain their health so that they can accomplish more and enjoy their achievements. The attitude you establish today will determine your success tomorrow. "For God has not given us a spirit of fear, but one of power, love, and sound judgment" (2 Timothy 1:7 CSB).

The great commandment tells us,

> …You shall love the Lord your God with all your heart, with all your soul, and with all your mind. This is the first and great commandment. And the second is like it: 'You shall love your neighbor as yourself.' On these two commandments hang all the Law and the Prophets.
>
> (Matthew 22:37–40 NKJV)

Imagine how we could impact each other if we all actively took this initiative— "…Love Thy Neighbor…" (Mark12:31 KJV). First, it would be in line with the word and what God wants us to do. Second, it would increase our circle of influence and support. It also would ensure someone is loving and checking on us since we are also someone's neighbor. Do you know your neighbors? If we each made an effort to get to know one neighbor in each direction—the neighbor in front of us, the neighbor behind us, and the neighbors to the left and to the right and checked on them routinely and helped them with what we could, what a difference we could make. Some might say that the church is supposed to take care of people. Guess what? We are the church! We can't help all, but we can each help some. Do your part. Get to know one another. If your immediate neighbors aren't receptive, go to the next house and watch your circle grow.

Love never loses its way home.

("Adinkra Symbols of West Africa" 2007c)

THE PRINCIPLE OF RESOURCEFULNESS

Scripture Ties:

And my God will meet all your needs according to his glorious riches in Christ Jesus.

(Philippians 4:19 KJV)

Bring the whole tithe into the storehouse, that there may be food in my house. Test me in this, says the LORD Almighty, and see if I will not throw open the floodgates of heaven and pour out so much blessing that you will not have room enough for it.

(Malachi 3:10 KJV)

For which of you, desiring to build a tower, does not first sit down and count the cost, whether he has enough to complete it?

(Luke 14:28 KJV)

For many people living the momentum, they can't even think of investing in a business because right now, they feel they can't even take care of business. To them, financial freedom is just the luxury of being able to spend money on something besides bills and necessities. There is only one thing you can do without money, and that is to think of ways to make money. However, there are three things you can do with money—you can spend it, you can manage it, or you can invest it. Financial freedom does not equal unlimited spending.

When you are poor, it seems to be spent as quickly as it is earned, and sometimes it is spent even before it is earned. When you are poor, money isn't there unless you can physically see it. There is no money sitting around in bank accounts. People keep it in cash, and they keep it with them. Money is real to them, and they spend it on real things. They are key strategists. They can maximize dollars in ways that most people can't imagine. They know that you can only spend a dollar once. They can't afford to waste it. Wasting it can mean the difference between eating or having a roof over their head or being able to get to work.

People with limited money face unimaginable pressure and seemingly impossible situations. I call it forced ingenuity. They know how to make a way out of no way.

I had no doubt that my youngest son would be a salesman. He loves to make money. When he was six-years-old, I walked into a room to witness him with a string tied around his tooth and the other end tied to the door. When I asked him what he was doing he said, "Did you know you can get money for these things?" I told him that I was aware of the customary tradition, but that usually we wait until they fall out. I then noticed that the string was tied around a tooth that was not even loose yet. When I brought this to his attention he said, "I know. I am going to pull them all!"

There is a simple key to money management—it is the fact that you can't manage without money! This key piece seems to elude many of us. I could not figure out how I appeared to have less money after my income had increased tenfold than when I was struggling with so much less. I then learned about the importance of tithing. If you give ten percent to God, it does come back to you tenfold! I am just mad at myself that my faith was not strong enough to realize this earlier in life.

My mother also gave me some good advice about money. She said that when you don't have much money, you spend until the money is spent, but when you think you have a little extra you spend until *you're* spent. My eyes were obviously bigger than my spending plan. *Don't let the pennies of today get in the way of the dollar signs in your future.*

> Money, if you use it, comes to an end; learning, if you use it, increases.
>
> ("2004 Weekly African Proverbs" 2004)

Remember:

> *You need to learn effective strategies to empower your money so that you can prosper.*

I've lived with money, and I've lived without it. Money doesn't buy happiness, but it buys choices. You need to make wise money decisions. I've learned that a good key to holding on to your hard-earned money is not to abandon the thrifty habits that you used out of necessity when you didn't have a lot of money coming in. Act your wage! Don't spend money you do not have.

A good way to keep money is to spend like you don't really have it. That is hard to do if you keep every bit of money you have in your wallet or on an easily accessible card. That temptation is often more than many of us can handle. So, remove the temptation and keep your money in an account that requires extra effort to access.

I keep my extra money in a savings account where I opt not to have a card that way, I have to physically go to the bank in order to access my money, and subsequently, I can only access it during banking hours. This method keeps me from compulsive spending, which I know is a weakness of mine. When I see something I want to buy, I first have to decide if it is truly worth the hassle of driving across town to the bank, then during the drive to the bank, I have even more time to consider the purchase. This method has stopped me from frivolous spending on many occasions.

Remember:

> *Manage your money instead of your money managing you.*

If you don't have credit cards, don't get credit cards. If you have credit cards, get rid of credit cards. Credit is so widespread and common that we take it for granted that it is a natural part of life, but in most countries, credit does not exist. If you want something, you save until you can get it or you live without it. I could not believe when I traveled to my husband's homeland that people had beautiful homes and cars, and credit was never an option. They paid cash! They live green because they don't have society telling them, through constant advertising, that they have to have the next, the best, and the newest. Look at all of the items we buy just to throw away—paper plates, cups, heavy-duty trash bags, and aluminum foil are just a few examples. What else? Look around your house and see what you can live without to put more money in your pocket.

I can remember one time I was so upset because my mop had broken and there were no replacement parts at the store. The Manager said that the replacement parts wouldn't be in until later the next week. So, I felt I had no choice but to wait. I came home a few days later, and my very dirty floor had been mopped. I asked my husband how he did it. He said with an old rag! I was so convinced that the only way to get my floors clean was by that special mop that I paralyzed myself from taking action. It was a simple solution for a simple problem that I had made complicated. Are you doing that? Are you making things more complicated than they need to be because you are convinced by something or someone that there is only one solution to a problem?

Poor is a personal definition based upon the standards you set. We tend to measure a quality life through material possessions, yet looks can be deceiving. Credit should be spelled 'credebt'. Debt = Doing Everything But Thinking.

It used to be easier to tell the "haves" from the "have nots". However, the widespread use of credit changed everything. Consider that your neighbor with a new car, new house, big-screen television may appear to be doing well but maybe having trouble keeping groceries in the refrigerator, keeping their utilities on, or putting gas in their cars because of the amount of loans that they are paying to keep all of those nice things.

Your neighbor knows you are alive but only you know how you are living.

("Africa's Proverb of the Day" 2018)

Once again, if you haven't started using credit, then don't, and if you are using credit then stop. It is a short time high with long term consequences. Avoid borrowing, if at all possible.

Remember:

> *God is not against you having money; he's against money having you. You cannot serve God and serve money. Proverbs 22:7 (NET) tells us, "The rich rule over the poor, and the borrower is servant to the lender."*

A good and simple budget model to follow is the 10–80–10 model. Ten percent is tithed as soon as you receive your money. Don't wait! Give that ten percent before you do anything else. The reason is you can never save your way toward quality living; you have to sow your way. Luke 6:38 (NIV) tells us, "Give, and it will be given to you. A good measure, pressed down, shaken together and running over, will be poured into your lap. For with the measure you use, it will be measured to you."

After you tithe, then use eighty percent of your income on your living expenses, and the remaining ten percent of your income can be placed in savings. (For every $100 that comes in tithe $10, spend $80 on your current expense and put the last $10 away).

10%   Tithe

80%   Current Expenses—Rent, Utilities, Car, Phone…

10%   Savings

Be sure to include fun things in your spending plan. For some reason, we feel that just because we have limited income, we shouldn't spend any money on activities or entertainment. What ultimately ends up happening when we do this is that we deprive ourselves of doing anything but work, home, pay bills, work, home pay bills (living life by the momentum) until sooner or later we get mentally overwhelmed and end up spending money we really don't have on impulse activities and then boom… we have a crisis with our finances. By putting activities and entertainment into the spending plan, we eliminate the possibility of "budget binging".

If you are not currently using the 10–80–10 model, you may have old debt that you need to pay off. Do not use your tithes to do this! Do not use the eighty percent that you are using to pay your current living expenses. Use five percent of the ten percent you have designated for savings each time you receive money to pay toward old debt until it is paid off then resume the 10–80–10 model.

Also, downloading an app to track your expenses on your phone can be very useful. It keeps you aware of where your money is going and helps you to identify areas that you need to tighten or adjust. If you do not have access to a phone app to track your expenses, then use good old paper, pencil, and a calculator. The *Stand Up!* website (www.standupinitiative.com) has downloadable 10–80–10 Budget Tracking worksheets available also.

When presenting *Stand Up!,* I ask participants what they would do with $1,000. Some of the responses have included: pay bills, put it in savings, or go on a vacation. After they get in small groups of five to ten and collectively decide what they would do with their combined money, the answers are vastly different: start a franchise, secure a bank loan, buy an existing business, invest in stocks and bonds, invest in real estate, buy money market CDs. Together they saw the benefit of empowering their money through collective economics and expanding their possibilities.

Look at this example… Take a simple bar of iron, it is worth $5. However, if you make it into a horseshoe, and it is worth about $50. Make it into needles, and it is worth about $500. Make it into springs for Swiss watches, and it could be worth half a million dollars. We need to learn to work with what we have in ways that are effective. How can you be resourceful?

Did you know that every year in the United States, Americans throw away over seven million pennies? Are you throwing away your talents? Are you throwing away parts of yourself that you don't think matter or add up to much? There is worth in everything that you do and everything that you are about.

Resourceful people do things differently than other people. They take chances and test their ideas. You must be willing to make mistakes, learn from them, and grow from them. Resourceful people will always find a way.

The next time you see a situation and you ask yourself, "What can I do?" rephrase it and ask yourself, "What can't I do?"

Remember:

> *All things are possible with God. "...If God is for us, who can be against us?" (Romans 8:31 NIV). It is time to get out of that comfort zone! Everyone wants convenience, but success is not convenient.*

Look at the areas on the *Stand Up! Quality Living Continuum*. Can you find ways to be resourceful in finding solutions to the needs that you identified? I eat out a lot, but I do not like to pay full price. I use coupons. I know the restaurants where kids eat free on different nights of the week, and I even participate once or twice a month in mystery shops where I am reimbursed for my meals along with a small stipend for my participation. I like to go to the stores that price match, so I can guarantee that I am paying the lowest price possible.

My husband has been handed down the tradition of bargaining. He is the only person I've ever seen negotiate prices on anything and everything. He has saved us literally thousands of dollars.

My mom and dad have a money habit where they never spend any of their change. Every time they break a dollar bill, they put the loose change away. Once a month, my dad will take the loose coins into the bank and deposit them into a savings club account. They have used this method to buy presents for all of their children and grandchildren for years!

Another good habit when you have a little extra cash is to buy your household necessities in bulk. You might hate spending the money at the time, but you will appreciate it during those times where you just don't have the extra to spend on the little things. Experiment with no-name brands also. There are some products that I refuse to compromise on, but others that I really can't tell the difference between the name brand and generic.

Another technique is bartering. Bartering is to exchange items or services without using money. Perhaps you don't have dependable transportation, but you love to cook, so you make a meal that you share with the neighbors every night, and they take you to and from work. See what talents, strengths, and abilities you may be able to barter for the things that you need.

Being resourceful also reduces waste, which is an important factor in our collective responsibility to our community. I'm sure that you have your own strategies. Please feel free to share them with others on the *Stand Up!* website (www.standupinitiative.com).

THE PRINCIPLE OF SELF DISCIPLINE

Scripture Ties:

For God gave us a spirit not of fear but of power and love and self-control.

(2 Timothy 1:7 ESV)

O Lord, your discipline is good and leads to life and health. Oh, heal me and make me live!

(Isaiah 38:16 TLB)

Even though it is great when we are able to take the initiative and be resourceful in our approach, we must exercise discipline in our actions. When you live life by the momentum everything appears to have a sense of urgency. When you decide a course of action make sure it is in line with the direction of your purpose and vision, you have support and cooperation, you have met your responsibilities, and that it is a financially sound decision.

You also must need to think of the amount of time that you spend on a course of action. We need to not only budget our money, but we need to budget our time. Everyone has the exact same amount of time each day. The only difference is how we spend it. How are you spending your time? Just like money, once it is spent you can't get it back. Spend your time wisely.

The things you do in your daily life can fall into four different categories:

> Category One —Things you do to keep yourself and your family safe and out of crisis. These are things that are important and urgent, and we need to dedicate time to manage them.

> Category Two —Things you do to better yourself, family, or situation. These may not be urgent, but they are important, and we need to focus on these things as they will help us *Stand Up!* and step toward a new direction!

Category Three —Things that are deceiving in that we feel like we need to do them, but they actually serve no practical purpose. These things are not important, but we often feel they are urgent. We need to try to limit these.

Category Four —Things that are a waste of our time but we do them anyway. These are not things that are important nor are they urgent. We should avoid these as much as possible.

Track your daily activities. The *Stand Up!* website (www.standupinitiative.com) has journal pages that you can use for this purpose. After a few days, review your activities to see what falls into category three or four. See if there are things you can change to better use your time and stay above the line.

CATEGORY ONE Important and Urgent	CATEGORY TWO Important and Necessary

CATEGORY THREE Perceived Urgent But Unimportant	CATEGORY FOUR Unimportant and Unnecessary

It takes discipline to change our negative behaviors, habits, and routines into positives. By planning how we can aggressively attack our challenging behaviors, habits, and routines, we can increase our chance of quality living. Knowing why we are passing on immediate gratification or satisfaction to achieve long term gains can help you resist temptation and lapsing into old practices.

It is here where we choose to:

- Curse it. ("Oh, I'll never be able to change this habit.")
- Nurse it. ("I'm going to change this habit eventually but not now.")
- Rehearse it. ("This is what it will be like once I change this habit.")
- Reverse it. ("I'm going to step toward a new direction!" and…)
- Rise above it!

Think of negative behaviors, habits, and routines that you wish you could change. You need to determine what motivates you to do them so that you can then determine how you can change them to be in line with your purpose and vision. Realize the reason you decide to stop a behavior, habit, or routine is not the same reason you started it.

Answer the following questions in regard to each individual behavior, habit, or routine that you would like to change. Be aware that each behavior, habit, or routine may have a different purpose behind it, so it is important to complete the questionnaire separately for each behavior, habit or routine and then address each one accordingly:

Personal Habits Motivation Questionnaire

1. Do you do this when you're alone?

2. Do you do it when you are bored?

3. Do you enjoy it?

4. When you are doing it, are you unaware of anything going on around you?

5. Do you do it when you have been given something difficult to do?

6. Do you do it when there is too much going on around you?

7. Do you do it to annoy or upset someone?

8. Do you do it when you feel you have a lot of demands on you?

9. Do you do it while talking and interacting with others?

10. Do you notice others observing you when you are doing it?

11. Do you do it when you feel lonely?

12. Do you do it to have someone spend time with you?

13. Do you do it to replace something you can't have or shouldn't do?

14. **Do you sneak to do it?**

15. Do you get upset if you don't get to do it?

16. Do you do it when you are disappointed or upset with someone or something?

If you answered "yes" to three out of four, in questions 1–4, then your behavior, habit, or routine is *emotional*. It is something that feels, looks, sounds, tastes, or smells good to you. It fills an internal void for you.

If you answered "yes" to three out of four answers, in questions 5–8, then your behavior, habit, or routine is *stress-related*. It is something you do to avoid or escape from people, places, or things and to reduce the demands of a situation. It is something you do when you feel trapped in a situation.

If you answered "yes" to three out of four answers, in questions 9–12, then your behavior, habit, or routine is *attention-seeking*. You want to obtain social attention or approval from someone.

If you answered "yes" to three out of four answers, in questions 13–16, then your behavior, habit, or routine occurs to obtain something *external* such as an object or favorite activity.

It is always easier to look for a solution to your behavior, habit, or routine without first interpreting the communication that it expresses. By learning the purpose that your behavior serves, you can then increase your chance of success in changing it or finding healthy alternatives. You may find that you have been unsuccessful in the past because you were dealing with the *symptoms* of your behavior, habit, or routine and not the *substance*. Now that you know the purpose they serve, you can begin developing goals to conquer them!

For instance, two of my friends both tried to stop vaping at the same time. They used the exact same techniques. However, only one of them was successful at first. After completing the *Personal Habits Motivation Questionnaire,* they discovered that they vaped for different reasons. My friend, who vaped for emotional reasons to fill an internal void, was able to substitute a healthier alternative that filled that void. She was able to quit vaping over time as her body adjusted to the healthier alternative. My friend, who vaped for stress-related reasons, did not get the stress relief that she wanted from the healthier alternative and, therefore, did not get the same results. After using the *Personal Habits Motivation Questionnaire,* she was able to tackle it a different way and eventually succeeded at kicking the habit.

Also, take into consideration that if you do not have a strong DNA match (Dedication, Necessity, and Acceptance of the outcomes) to a behavior, habit, or routine, then you won't be successful in changing it, so recognize this and focus on the things you feel strongly committed to change. Sometimes behaviors and habits can take a dark turn and develop into addictions. Do not be afraid to ask for help if changing your behavior, habit, or routine is not something that you can do on your own.

Remember:

When in doubt, reach out!

There are resources available on the Stand Up! website (www.standupinitiative.com).

TIME FOR ACTION

Scripture Ties:

Each morning I will look to you in heaven and lay my requests before you, praying earnestly.

(Psalm 5:3 TLB)

Reserve daily time with God for reflection on your activity and what you have chosen "to do," always ensuring it is in line with the Word. Write your favorite comfort scriptures in your *Stand Up!* journal and read them daily available through the *Stand Up!* website (www.standupinitiative.com). If you have not yet completed the *Stand Up! Quality Living Continuum,* please do so now. The continuum will help you determine priority areas to address as you continue on your journey. You must examine your life areas to find the areas that must be addressed when setting realistic goals. It is time for you to take action! It is time for you to *Stand Up! For Yourself.*

By now you have defined a new direction, you have developed your purpose and vision statement, you know the principles to guide you in that new direction and have identified the changes that you want to make. Now, you will need to decide how you will do this. This is where you will develop your action plan.

We often think about things that we would like to improve; we think about goals we would like to achieve, but how many of us actually write them down and track our progress? In order to be proactive instead of reactive, we need to use stepping stones to achieve our goals.

Remember:

> *The hardest part of achieving a goal is getting started. If you don't set a goal you will hit it every time! Look for goals that will not only inspire you but perspire you (make you work for it!)*

Almost everyone has some form of planner where they write down their appointments, their calls to make, their prioritized "To Do" lists. However, on mine, I also write down my purpose and vision statement and identify what area of wellbeing I am addressing, so I can ensure I stay balanced. I also ask myself with each entry I make on my "To Do" list, "Is this important and if so, to whom?" Be sure that what you are doing is purposeful and is in line with the goals that you have defined.

It is also important to keep a journal. It is a great way not only to track your progress but can be an opportunity to relieve the stresses of the day. Put any negativity on paper and be done with it. Additionally, journals are a wonderful way to track major events in your life. My mother would write every childhood illness that any of us had in the front of our old family Bible. She also wrote births, weddings, and deaths. It was her designated spot. Your journal can be your designated spot to track anything and everything that happens in your family. It is your place to record celebrations and tribulations.

There are many planner apps that you can download on your phone or computer. However, I prefer a planner that I can physically carry with me and write in. My collection of planners over the years is not only an action plan for my here-and-now but a journal of my past challenges and accomplishments. I keep them to reflect and remind myself of how far I've come. It is something that I will pass down in my family just like a photo album. If you also prefer the written page over a phone app., visit the *Stand Up!* website (www.standupinitiative.com).

Visit the *Stand Up!* website (www.standupinitiative.com) to access all of the resources to help you remember your commitment to step toward a new direction using principles. You will be able to see constant reminders of *Stand Up!* each day. You will be able to organize your comfort scriptures and confirm your daily devotions, as well as record your day-to-day activities, identify your circle of support, track your 10–80–10 Budget Plan, identify your "Household Responsibility and ICU Checklist," celebrate your "Blessings In The Storms," record your "Celebrations and Tribulations," journalize your events and identify new ideas but will also help you establish your goals all in one location!

STAND UP! GOAL SETTING

Scripture Ties:

Let us search out and examine our ways, and turn back to the Lord.

(Lamentations 3:40 NKJV)

But when he, the Spirit of truth, comes, he will guide you into all the truth. He will not speak on his own; he will speak only what he hears, and he will tell you what is yet to come.

(John 16:13 NIV)

***Stand Up!* Goal-Setting Strategies:**

S = Set your goals.

T = Target your goal area.

A = Analyze your goal type.

N = Navigate your action steps.

D = Determine methods and timeframes.

U = Utilize your tools.

P = Progress toward your goal.

Set Your Goals

First, you must identify your goals. You may already have some goals in mind, or you can use areas from the *Stand Up! Quality Living Continuum,* the *Health Awareness Appraisal,* or the *Personal Habit Motivation Questionnaire* that you completed in earlier sections.

After identifying the areas in which you would like to action, you will then develop your goal statements. A goal statement should contain three things:

- An action that is to take place.
- A single trackable result.
- A timeline for completion.

A goal statement should be short and to the point. A goal statement should not conflict with your purpose and vision. A goal statement should be something that will challenge you, be meaningful, and important to you so that you will try to accomplish it and stick with it until you do.

Your goal statement will say what you are going to do and how long it is going to take you. As we discussed under the principle of "Responsibility," you should have a strong DNA match to your goal statements! Is it something you can *dedicate* yourself too? Do you feel it is *necessary* for you to achieve this goal? Is this goal *acceptable* to you?

Target Your Goal Area

After identifying your goal statements, decide where it best fits in your overall wellbeing that was identified in the *Stand Up! Quality Living Continuum*:

➤ Personal/Interpersonal Wellbeing (about my family and me)

Examples of personal/interpersonal goals:

- I will join the gym to improve my health.
- I will make the entire family appointments at the doctor and dentist for check-ups.

➤ Financial Wellbeing (about our money/spending plan, our jobs)

Examples of financial goals:

- I will carpool to work.
- I will track all of my expenses on my 10–80–10 Budget Tracker.

- Material Wellbeing (about our house, food, transportation, household, and personal necessities)

   Examples of material goals:

   - I will buy food to pack lunches for school and work.
   - I will make a list to take to the store to prevent impulse buying.

- Social Wellbeing (about my friends, relatives, co-workers, classmates, and acquaintances)

   Examples of social goals:

   - I will have critical ICU time with my family.
   - I will take the family to a community event.

- Spiritual Wellbeing (about my faith community)

   Examples of spiritual goals:

   - I will read daily devotions.
   - I will attend a *Stand Up! Life Group.*

Analyze Your Goal Type (How long is this goal going to take you?)

After developing your goal statements, you will identify the type of goal:

- Is it a *short-term goal* with an expected result that you will be able to see within the next year? (For example, I want to exercise three times each week.)

- Is it a *routine goal* that is not time-limited that you just want to remind yourself by tracking? (For example, I have a routine goal to take my vitamins each morning.)

- Is it a *long-range goal* that you hope to accomplish within the next two to five years? (For example, I want to own my own house.)

- Is it a *wish-list goal* that you can't start yet but want to make sure that you write it down because you can see yourself doing it in the future? (For example, I want to own my own business.)

Navigate Your Action Steps to Achieve Your Goal (What You Are Going "To Do"?)

After you develop your goal statement, identify your goal area, and establish your goal type, you will set action steps to achieve it. This will tell you what you are going to do. Be sure to take into consideration the motivation behind your behavior, habit or routine that you learned from taking the *Personal Habits Motivation Questionnaire*. Do you do it because of emotional reasons, stress, to get attention, or because it is something that is rewarding to you? This will help you in determining the right action steps to take.

Determine Methods (How) and Time Frames (When)

You want to take action on your goals, so setting steps showing how you are going to work on your goal and when you are going to work on your goal is very important.

Utilize Your Tools to Start Your Goal

It is not only important to set a time for when you would like to have your goal achieved, but it is also important to determine how soon you are going to get started. Don't procrastinate! Start as soon as possible.

Remember:

> *You are living life by the moment and deciding what is important to you instead of living life by the momentum. Saying you are too busy is not acceptable! Those days are over!*

Progress Toward Your Goal

You should check your progress frequently. If you don't see you are making progress, then you may need to review your goal and revise your action steps so that you can see the progress toward your expected results.

Remember:

> *Never stop! If you experience setbacks change the date, don't change the goal.*

The *Stand Up!* website (www.standupinitiative.com) has goal sheets available, or you can develop your own. The important thing is that you get started. It's time to *Stand Up!* Step Toward A New Direction! and achieve your goals. Just think how great you are going to feel when you have accomplished what you set out TO DO!

Set New Goals!

Remember:

> *It's a life-long journey, not a final destination; keep stepping toward that new direction.*

WHAT'S NEXT

Scripture Ties:

'For I know the plans I have for you,' declares the Lord, 'plans to prosper you and not to harm you, plans to give you hope and a future.'

(Jeremiah 29:11 NIV)

Jesus said to him, 'If you can believe, ^{all things} *are* possible to him who believes.'

(Mark 9:23 NKJV)

Being confident of this, that he who began a good work in you will carry it on to completion until the day of Christ Jesus.

(Philippians 1:6 NIV)

There is a story that I heard many years ago about a man who was employed by a road crew that paints the middle lines on the highway. On his first day, his enthusiasm was met with great praise from his supervisor. On his second day, the supervisor again was pleased with his performance. However, the supervisor noticed that he had slowed down somewhat. By the third day, the supervisor began seeing flaws in the paint job. The lines were swaying all over the road, and by the fourth day, hardly any work had been completed at all. The Supervisor confronted the man about his performance, "Why when you were doing so well at the beginning, am I now seeing such poor performance?" The man looking defensive replied, "Hey! It's a long walk back to that paint bucket!"

Don't be like the man in the story. Don't keep going all the way back to the beginning. You must remember to keep stepping forward and to take your tools and resources with you. It is time to paint a new picture of your life. A picture of quality living! *Stand Up! For Yourself and Step Toward a New Direction Using Principles.*

Remember:

> *As you start down the road, don't try to visit yesterday to get things done—yesterday is never coming back. Don't try to visit tomorrow to get it done-tomorrow never comes. Today is the time to do it! The time is now for you to translate your purpose and vision into action!*

What is YOUR action plan after today? How will you achieve your purpose and vision? Write the following on your calendar. Ten days from today, "What have I done to *Stand Up!* for myself?" Twenty days from today write, "Am I tracking my progress? Thirty days from today, "How am I doing?" And three months from today write, "Time to review my plan."

It is time to get it out of your head and into your heart. Take at least one step toward a new direction today if you haven't done so already. From there, the possibilities are endless. Below are some suggestions for what's next:

- Begin applying the *Stand Up!* principles in your life and the lives of your family.

- Share *Stand Up!* with your friends, family, and faith community.

- Share the *Stand Up! Quality Living Continuum* as an outreach program in your community or church.

- Start tracking your 10–80–10 budget.

- Begin your *Stand Up!* Gloats, Quotes, and *Journal Notes*.

- Begin your *Stand Up! Goal Tracking*.

- Begin using the *Household Responsibility and ICU checklist* from the *Stand Up!* website (www.standupinitiative.com).

- Start or join a *Stand Up! Life Group, Support Group*, or *Community Group* to enlarge your circle of support as well as your circle of influence.

- Expand your network of resources. Find out what services and supports are available in your community and share the information.

- Love Thy Neighbor by getting to know those who live in your community.

- Educate yourself. Take online courses, sign up for

a class at a local school, or college, and utilize the resources at the library and online.

- Visit the *Stand Up!* website (www.standupinitiative.com) and share your successes with others.

Don't get discouraged if you run into roadblocks. Persevere! Keep pursuing your goals. Don't give up—have faith! Most importantly, *Stand Up!* whatever you have committed to do—DO IT!

And as a final note, I ask that you help me reach one of my goals by doing the following—share the *Stand Up!* program with friends and family and pass this book along to someone else who can benefit from it.

He who does not know can know from learning.

("Adinkra Symbols of West Africa" 2007d)

APPENDIX

STAND UP! INITIATIVE
Quality Living Continuum
On the Path from Bondage to Abundance
Circle the sentences that best identify you or your family's current situation

CONTROL KEY AREAS	PATHWAY ONE	PATHWAY TWO	PATHWAY THREE	PATHWAY FOUR	PATHWAY FIVE
PHYSICAL AND MENTAL HEALTH	• One or more of us need some type of treatment or medication now. • We don't have insurance.	• We don't attend regular appointments. • We only address our health when it becomes a crisis. • We usually go to urgent care facilities. • We do not have adequate health coverage and/or we can't pay our co-pay or deductible.	• We go to the doctor but not regularly. • We have health coverage, but we only use it as a last resort.	• We keep our appointments, but it is sometimes difficult with our co-pay or deductible. • We have adequate health coverage for now.	• We have an established routine of preventative medical care. • We have routine caregivers. • We are all covered by affordable, adequate health insurance.
COMMUNITY CONNECTIONS	• We don't have anyone to help us. • We don't have a phone or any means to contact people. • There is a language barrier.	• Our family and friends are supportive, but they don't have the resources or time to help us. • We don't have a phone or have limited ways to contact people. • We do not speak English that well or understand what others are saying at times.	• We have some support from family, but it is not consistent or dependable. • We don't always have access to a phone or a way to contact people. • English is not our first language, so sometimes this makes it difficult.	• We have support from family or friends. • We have a phone and/or a consistent way to contact people. • There is no language barrier.	• We have family and friends that help us, and we are able to help them if needed. • We have multiple ways to contact people. • There is no language barrier.

JENNIE MSANGI

CONTROL KEY AREAS	PATHWAY ONE	PATHWAY TWO	PATHWAY THREE	PATHWAY FOUR	PATHWAY FIVE
HOUSING	• We are homeless. • We are being evicted. • We are staying with family or friends.	• We have housing, but it isn't permanent. • We have housing, but it is too small. • We have housing, but it isn't a safe place. • We worry about eviction every month.	• We have housing, but we don't feel safe in the neighborhood. • We have housing, but it isn't big enough and/or needs repair.	• We have housing that we can afford and it meets our needs.	• We have housing that we like, and we can afford it. • We own our house.
FOOD	• We don't have food or food assistance. • We rely on others for food. • We often go without or eat food we wouldn't eat if we had other choices.	• We have food assistance but have limited ways and times to get to the store. • We run out before the next month. • We buy fast food out of convenience. • We go to local food pantries to get by.	• We have food assistance and can fix it. • We are limited in what we can eat because it is all we can afford. • We sometimes go to the food pantry.	• We can meet basic food needs. • We don't go hungry.	• We can purchase any food our household desires. • We eat when and what we want.

CONTROL KEY AREAS	PATHWAY ONE	PATHWAY TWO	PATHWAY THREE	PATHWAY FOUR	PATHWAY FIVE
TRANSPORTATION	• We have no access to dependable transportation.	• We have transportation, but it is not always available, unreliable, unpredictable, unaffordable. • We have a car but no car insurance. • We don't have a licensed driver in the house.	• We have transportation, but it is limited or inconvenient at times. • We don't have adequate car insurance.	• We can meet our basic transportation needs.	• Transportation is readily available, and an affordable car is adequately insured.
HOUSE-HOLD AND PERSONAL NECESSITIES	• We aren't able to get the things we need. • We don't have clothes that fit or are adequate for school or work.	• We are only able to get a few of our household and personal necessities right now and not consistently.	• We can get most but not all of our household and personal necessities with assistance.	• We can get basic household and personal necessities without assistance.	• We are able to choose and purchase the personal and household necessities that we prefer.
MONEY / BUDGET	• We don't have any income right now. • We have money coming in, but it is sporadic and not dependable.	• We have income, but it isn't enough to meet our bills and our needs/wants. • We use payday loans.	• We have an income to pay the bills but nothing for extras, and if we had any type of reduction, we would lose it all.	• We have enough income to pay the bills and cover most of our wants.	• Our income is sufficient, and we have an adequate amount of savings.

CONTROL KEY AREAS	PATHWAY ONE	PATHWAY TWO	PATHWAY THREE	PATHWAY FOUR	PATHWAY FIVE
EMPLOYMENT / EDUCATION	• No one is working right now. • No one is able to work right now. • One or more adults in our household need to obtain GED/Diploma.	• We are working, but it is temporary, part-time, or seasonal. • We work, but it isn't enough and no benefits. • One or more adults are attending classes for a GED/diploma.	• We are working, but the pay is not enough, and we get little or no benefits. • At least one person in our household has a GED/diploma.	• We have jobs with enough pay to cover our bills, and we have benefits. • We have GED/diploma and/or college.	• We have permanent employment with enough income and benefits to maintain our household. • We have completed training/college after high school.
CHILDCARE / ELDERCARE	• We need childcare/eldercare, but it isn't available, accessible, or our family is not eligible.	• We have childcare/eldercare, but it is unreliable or unaffordable. • We are worried about the level of supervision and care our family member is getting.	• We have childcare/eldercare, but it is limited, and if it wasn't subsidized or with family, we couldn't make it.	• We have reliable, affordable childcare/eldercare. • We don't need any subsidies.	• We have quality childcare/eldercare of our choice. • We do not have childcare/eldercare needs at this time.
LEGAL ISSUES	• One or more of us have outstanding tickets, warrants, or an open case.	• One or more of us have current charges/trial pending, noncompliance with probation/parole. • Prior convictions that limit our choices.	• One or more of us are on probation/parole but are compliant.	• One or more of us have had a legal issue in the past, but it does not affect anything now.	• We do not have any legal issues.

CONTROL KEY AREAS	PATHWAY ONE	PATHWAY TWO	PATHWAY THREE	PATHWAY FOUR	PATHWAY FIVE
OUR CHILDREN'S EDUCATION	• Our school-age child(ren) are not enrolled in school.	• Our school-age child(ren) are enrolled but not attending class, or I have trouble getting them there.	• Our school-age child(ren) are in school, but sometimes they do not attend, or we have to send them even when they are sick because we don't have any alternatives.	• Our school-age child(ren) go to school regularly.	• Our school-age child(ren) go to school without any issues at a school of our choice. • We don't have any school-age children at this time.
SPIRITUAL	• We can't worry about that right now.	• We would like to know more about options or how to get involved in the faith community, but we aren't sure where to start.	• We have some faith community connections, but it is only occasionally, or there are transportation or childcare issues or conflicts with work schedules.	• We know some of what is available, and we know how to get involved with our faith community.	• We are active participants in our faith community.

CONTROL KEY AREAS	PATHWAY ONE	PATHWAY TWO	PATHWAY THREE	PATHWAY FOUR	PATHWAY FIVE
KEY TO YOUR OVERALL PROSPERITY	If you circled anything on ROAD ONE... • You are living in bondage in that area. • You do not have to do this anymore! • Let us help you find resources to move you out of the area.	If you circled anything on ROAD TWO... • Then you are living life by the momentum! • You are spinning your wheels! • You don't have to keep struggling. • Let us help you find solutions to move you to the next level.	If you circled anything on ROAD THREE... • Then you are stuck at a crossroads in that area. • You are living in survival mode. • Let us help you STAND UP! And step towards a new direction.	If you circled anything on ROAD FOUR... • Then you are safe for now. • We all have room for improvement. • Let us help you set goals to take it the rest of the way!	If you circled anything on ROAD FIVE... • Then you are living an abundant life! • You are not just surviving your thriving in that area! • Now would be a good time to see what you can do for the people who circled things in the other 4 levels of living.

REFERENCES

"2004 Weekly African Proverbs." 2004. Afriprov.Org. 2004. https://www.afriprov.org/weekly-african-proverbs/250-2004-weekly-african-proverbs.html.

"Adinkra Symbols of West Africa." 2007a. Adinkra.Org. 2007. http://www.adinkra.org/htmls/adinkra/wawa.htm.

———. "Adinkra Symbols of West Africa." 2007b. Adinkra.Org. 2007. http://www.adinkra.org/htmls/adinkra/boame.htm.

———. "Adinkra Symbols of West Africa." 2007c. Adinkra.Org. 2007. http://www.adinkra.org/htmls/adinkra/odon.htm.

———. "Adinkra Symbols of West Africa." 2007d. Adinkra.Org. 2007. http://www.adinkra.org/htmls/adinkra/neao.htm.

"Africa's Proverb of the Day." 2018. BBC News. 2018. https://www.bbc.com/news/world-africa-18930368.

"Chinese Proverb." n.d. Quotes.Net. Accessed November 15, 2019. https://www.quotes.net/quote/9106.

"Diversity Shirts." 2019. TheNthDegree.Com. 2019. http://www.thenthdegree.com/diversity.asp.

"Ganda (Uganda) Proverb." n.d. African Proverbs. Accessed November 15, 2019. https://www.afriprov.org/african-proverb-of-the-month/32-2006proverbs/232-december-2006-proverb-qunity-is-strengthq-ganda-uganda-.html.

"Inspirational and Motivational Quotes: Anonymous Simplified Version of 'A Poem About Responsibility' by Charles Osgood." 2019. Buisnessballs. 2019. https://www.businessballs.com/amusement-stress-relief/quotes-inspirational-motivational/#the-everybody-somebody-anybody-nobody-story-or-poem-.

"Jefferson Ruritan Club." 2016. Larry Cassell.

Kearney, Mike. 2011. "Drownproofing." 2011. http://www.drownproofing.com/.

"Kenyan Proverb." n.d. PassItOn.Com. Accessed November 15, 2019. https://www.passiton.com/inspirational-quotes/4421-sticks-in-a-bundle-are-unbreakable.

McDougall, Christopher. 2009. *Born to Run : A Hidden Tribe, Superathletes, and the Greatest Race the World Has Never Seen.* Alfred A. Knopf.

"Principle." 2019. Dictionary.Com. 2019. https://www.dictionary.com/browse/principle?s=t.

"Quote by Edward Everett Hale." 2019. BrainyQuote. 2019. https://www.brainyquote.com/quotes/edward_everett_hale_121997.

"Quote by Haim G. Ginott." 2019. Goodreads.Com. 2019. https://www.goodreads.com/quotes/59581-i-have-come-to-the-frightening-conclusion-that-i-am.

"Quote by John Bradford." 2019. This Day in Quotes. 2019. http://www.thisdayinquotes.com/2011/07/there-but-for-grace-of-god-goes-john.html.

"Quote by Moosa Rahat." 2019. Goodreads.Com. 2019. https://www.goodreads.com/quotes/7655885-show-me-your-friends-and-i-ll-show-you-your-future.

"Quote by Ralph Waldo Emerson." 2019. Goodreads. 2019. https://www.goodreads.com/quotes/511854-sorrow-looks-back-worry-looks-around-faith-looks-up.

"Quote by Roy T. Bennett:" 2019. Goodreads.Com. 2019. https://www.goodreads.com/quotes/7973140-don-t-let-others-tell-you-what-you-can-t-do-don-t.

"Quote by St. Jerome." 2019. Brainy Quote. 2019. https://www.brainyquote.com/quotes/st_jerome_389605.

"Quote from Field of Dreams." 2019. Wikiquote. 2019. https://en.wikiquote.org/wiki/Field_of_Dreams.

"Swahili Wisdom about Patience." 2019. Quotecover.Com. 2019. https://quotescover.com/swahili-proverb-about-patience.

The Good News Bible [GNT]. 1966, 1971, 1976, 1992. New

York: American Bible Society. https://www.biblegateway.com/versions/Good-News-Translation-GNT-Bible/#booklist

The Holy Bible: Amplified Bible Classic [AMPC]. 1954, 1958, 1962, 1964, 1965, 1967, 1987. The Lockman Foundation. https://www.biblegateway.com/versions/Amplified-Bible-Classic-Edition-AMPC/#copy

The Holy Bible: Common English Bible [CEB]. 1976, 1998. https://www.biblegateway.com/versions/Common-English-Bible-CEB/#copy

The Holy Bible: English Standard Version [ESV]. 2007. Wheaton, Ill: Crossway Bibles. Public Domain. https://www.biblegateway.com/versions/English-Standard-Version-ESV-Bible/#booklist

The Holy Bible: King James Version [KJV]. 1999. New York: American Bible Society. Public Domain. https://www.biblegateway.com/versions/King-James-Version-KJV-Bible/#booklist

The Holy Bible: New American Standard Bible [NASB]. 1960, 1962, 1963, 1968, 1971, 1972, 1973, 1975, 1977, 1995, The Lockman Foundation. http://www.lockman.org/nasb/index.php

The Holy Bible: New English Translation [NET]. 1996-2006. Biblical Studies Press. https://www.biblegateway.com/versions/New-English-Translation-NET-Bible/#vinfo

The Holy Bible: New International Version [NIV]. 1984. Grand Rapids: Zondervan Publishing House. https://www.biblegateway.com/versions/New-International-Version-NIV-Bible/#booklist

The Holy Bible: The Christian Standard Bible [CSB]. 2017. Holman Bible Publishers. https://www.biblegateway.com/versions/Christian-Standard-Bible-CSB/#copy

The Holy Bible: The New King James Version [NKJV]. 1999, Nashville: Thomas Nelson. https://www.biblegateway.com/versions/New-King-James-Version-NKJV-Bible/#booklist

The Holy Bible: The Living Bible [TLB]. 1971, Carol Stream, Illinois: Tyndale House Publishers, Inc.

The Holy Bible: New Living Translation [NLT]. 1996, 2994, 2997, 2013. Tyndale House Foundation. Carol Stream, Illinois: Tyndale House Publishers, Inc. https://www.biblegateway.com/versions/New-Living-Translation-NLT-Bible/#booklist

"Universal Declaration of Human Rights." n.d. United Nations. Accessed November 15, 2019. https://www.un.org/en/universal-declaration-human-rights/.

Zimmerman, Alan. 2016. "What You Speak About You Bring About - Positive Communication Pro." Dr. Zimmerman. Com. 2016. https://www.drzimmerman.com/blog/what-you-speak-about-you-bring-about.

ABOUT THE AUTHOR

Jennie and her husband, Gill, have committed their lives to serve God by serving others. Together they have five children and twelve grandchildren. Their youngest child, Mary Faith, still lives at home.

Jennie has earned a Master's degree in Education Administration and holds a Bachelor of Arts in Business Management. She has over thirty years of public service experience. She says that **Stand Up!** was developed to reach individuals and families in the community who may not otherwise be aware of the available resources or have the tools needed to live prosperously and achieve overall wellbeing.

Gill's charismatic personality and influence from his homeland of Tanzania, East Africa have been inspirational in providing a varied perspective. One of which is African sayings, proverbs, and symbols that have been interwoven throughout **Stand Up!** to enrich the participant's experience.

The logo used for **Stand Up!** shows arrows pointing inwards from all directions to the cross at the center. No matter what direction you are coming from, you can't go wrong if your new direction is focused on Jesus. With Him, all things are possible! Stand Up! For Yourself it is time.

CPSIA information can be obtained
at www.ICGtesting.com
Printed in the USA
LVHW050744270420
654450LV00011B/1016